CAMP COOKERY

By
HORACE KEPHART

Author of
Camping and Woodcraft, The Hunting
Rifle, etc.

Illustrated With Pen Drawings of Camp Utensils,
Outfits, etc.

Cornerstone Book Publishers
New Orleans, LA

Camp Cookery
by Horace Kephart

A Cornerstone Book
Published by Cornerstone Book Publishers
An Imprint of Michael Poll Publishing
Copyright © 2013 by Cornerstone Book Publishers

Cornerstone Book Publishers
New Orleans, LA

First Cornerstone Edition - 2013

www.cornerstonepublishers.com

ISBN: 1613420862
ISBN-13: 978-1-61342-086-7

MADE IN THE USA

FOREWORD.

The less a man carries in his pack, the more he must carry in his head.

A camper cannot go by recipe alone. It is best for him to carry sound general principles in his head, and recipes in his pocket.

The simpler the outfit, the more skill it takes to manage it, and the more pleasure one gets in his achievements.

CONTENTS.

CAMP COOKERY

A TABLE.

All recipes in this book are here grouped under *Quick, Medium,* or *Slow,* according to the time they take. Everything under *Quick* can be prepared in less than 25 minutes, and so is specially suitable for breakfast or luncheon.

The table also shows at a glance what recipes call for milk, butter, or eggs, and what do not. The following abbreviations are used:

E = Eggs required (whole or desiccated).
B = Butter required.
M = Milk required (may be evaporated or powdered).
E*= Eggs desirable, but may be omitted.
B*= Butter desirable, but other fat may be substituted.
M*= Milk desirable, but water may be substituted.
¶ = Made over from previously boiled material.

QUICK.
(*Under 25 minutes.*)

xi

MEDIUM.
(25 to 45 minutes.)

Fresh Meat, Game.

Fish.

Shellfish, etc.

Cured Meats.

Camp Cookery

CHAPTER I.

PROVISIONS.

THE knack of camp outfitting consists in getting the best kit in the least weight and bulk. Wise campers prefer to go light, doing without most of the appliances of domestic life. It follows that camp cookery is an art distinct from the cuisine of kitchens. A common cook-book is of no use in the woods; for it is always calling for things we have not, and does not tell what to do with the things we have.

For example, I am to make a side trip of several days from the main camp. Going alone, and without pack horse or canoe, I must cut down my equipment to the last practicable ounce. There will be neither time nor utensils for baking on the way. So I must have bread for the journey, and it must be wholesome bread, extra nourishing for its bulk, palatable, fit to eat cold, and of a kind that will not dry out nor mould. I have no materials but flour, salt, sugar, baking powder, and water. Where shall I find the recipe? Not in a

1

domestic cook-book. Yet the trick is easy, when one knows how.

Light outfitting, as regards food, is mainly a question of *how much water* we are willing to carry in our rations. For instance, canned peaches are 88 per cent. water. Can one afford to carry so much water from home when there is better water at camp? What, then, is best to substitute for the peaches? Let us see.—

An average can of peaches weighs 2½ lbs. Evaporated apples are only 26 per cent. water, and sugar has none at all. A pound of the apples and a pound of sugar cost three-fourths as much as the peaches, weigh a fifth less, are a little bulkier, but pack better on the trail. In camp, let the apples be stewed soft in plenty of water, and used as sauce. There is left a quart of hot juice. Into it put the pound of sugar. Boil, without stirring or skimming, until the juice gets syrupy, and pour into a vessel to cool. Result: somewhat more than a pint of as good jelly as can be made from fresh apples themselves. The sauce and the jelly will go much farther than a can of peaches, and there is more variety.

The following table is suggestive:

More than ¾ Water.
Fresh milk, fruit, vegetables (except potatoes).
Canned soups, tomatoes, peaches, pears, etc.

More than ½ Water.
Fresh beef, veal, mutton, poultry, eggs, potatoes.
Canned corn, baked beans, pineapple.
Evaporated milk (unsweetened).

More than ⅓ Water.
Fresh bread, rolls, pork chops.
Potted chicken, etc.
Cheese.
Canned blackberries.

Less than ⅓ Water.

Dried apples, apricots, peaches, prunes.
Fruit jelly.

Less than ⅕ Water.

Salt pork (fat). Dried fish. Butter.
Desiccated eggs. Concentrated soups.
Powdered milk.
Wheat flour, corn meal, etc. Macaroni.
Rice, oatmeal, hominy, etc.
Dried beans, split peas.
Dehydrated vegetables.
Dried dates, figs, raisins.
Orange marmalade. Sugar. Chocolate.
Nuts. Nut butter.

Although this table is good in its way, it is not
a fair measure of the relative value of foods.
Even the solid part of some foodstuffs contains a
good deal of refuse (fresh potatoes 20 per cent.),
while others have none. Beans, rice, nuts, cheese,
are highly concentrated foods, but rice is easy to
digest, beans rather difficult, nuts more so (unless
in the form of nut butter), and cheese should be
used sparingly. Then there is the personal factor: "What's one man's meat is another man's
poison."

Variety is quite as welcome at the camp board
as anywhere else—in fact more so, for it is harder
to get. Do not leave out the few little condiments wherewith you can vary the taste of common articles and serve a new sauce or gravy or
pudding now and then. Nothing pays better for
its transportation than *good* brands of desiccated
eggs and evaporated or powdered milk. Cooked
in combination with other things, they add vastly
to the number and savor of your dishes.

There is an old school of campers who affect
to scorn such things. "We take nothing with us,"
they say, "but pork, flour, baking powder, salt,

sugar, and coffee—our guns and rods furnish *us*
variety." This sounds sturdy, but there is a deal
of humbug in it. A spell of bad weather may de-
feat the best of hunters and fishermen. Even
granting that luck is good, the kill is likely to be
of one kind at a time. With only the six articles
named, nobody can serve the same game in a variety of ways. Now, consider a moment. How
would you like to sit down to nothing but fried
chicken and biscuit, three times a day? Chicken
everlastingly fried in pork grease—and, if you
tire of that, well, eat fried "sow-belly," and sop
your bread in the grease! It is just the same with
trout or bass as it is with chicken; the same with
pheasant or duck, rabbit or squirrel or bear. The
only kind of wild meat that civilized man can relish
for three consecutive meals, served in the same
fashion, is venison of the deer family. Go prepared to lend variety to your menu. Food that
palls is bad food—worse in camp than anywhere
else, for you can't escape to a restaurant.

Variety of rations does not mean. adding to the
load. It means *substituting* three 5 lb. parcels for
one 15 lb. parcel, and no more.

Let us consider the material of field rations, item
by item:

Bread.—It may be well to carry enough yeast
bread for two or three days. It helps out until
the game country is reached and camp routine
is established. Hardtack (pilot bread, ship biscuit) is a last resort, and can be recommended only
for such trips or cruises as do not permit baking.
It is a cracker prepared without salt or grease, and
kiln-dried to a chip, so as to keep well. He who
can eat it without grumbling may be said to have
filed his teeth.

Flour.—The plain kind is best. The self-raising is easily ruined by moisture, and will not do for thickening, dredging, etc.

Corn Meal.—Some like yellow, some prefer white. In either case it is much the best when freshly ground. A welcome change from hot wheat bread or biscuit, and can be served variously as johnny cake, pancakes, or mush. Useful to roll fish in, before frying.

Rolled Oats.—This, and other breakfast cereals, according to taste, and only for variety sake. Nutritive value low, in proportion to bulk.

Rice.—Deserves a higher place as an all-round food than our people generally give it. Beats all other cereals in sustaining power plus digestibility. Can be cooked in many ways, and all of them are easy. Combines well with almost anything else, and so lends variety. Packs well and keeps well.

Macaroni.—Nutritious, but bulky. Good in soups and stews. Break it into inch pieces and pack so that insects cannot get at it.

Baking Powder.—Get the best, made with pure cream of tartar. It costs more than the alum powders, and does not go so far, bulk for bulk; but it is much kinder to the stomach. Baking soda will probably not be wanted, as it requires buttermilk in baking, except for sour-dough. Occasionally needed for other purposes.

Salt Pork (*alias* middlings, sides, bellies, Old Ned, *et al.*).—Commendable or accursed, according to how it is used. Takes the place of lard and butter on very light marching trips. Nothing quite equals it in baking beans. Savory in some boiled dishes. When fried, as a *pièce de résistance,* it successfully resists most people's gastric juices, and is nauseous to many. Purchasable at most frontier camps.

Breakfast Bacon.—Better for most purposes than salt pork. Seldom obtainable outside of towns. Get the boneless, in 5 to 8 lb. flitches. That which is sliced and canned is a poor substitute either in flavor or wholesomeness.

Smoked Ham.—Small ones generally are tough and too salty. Hard to keep in warm or damp weather; moulds easily, and is attractive to blow-flies. It is best to get both bacon and ham un-wrapped, and sew them up in cheesecloth yourself; then you are sure they were not mouldy to start with.

Dried Beef.—Cuts from large hams are best. Of limited use in pick-up meals. A notorious thirst-breeder. Not comparable to "jerked" beef, which, unfortunately, is not in the market.*

Canned Meats and Poultry of all descriptions are quite unfit for steady diet. Devilled or potted ham, chicken, tongue, sausage, and the like, are endurable at picnics, and valuable in emergencies, as when a hard storm makes outdoor cooking impossible. Canned corned beef makes a passable hash.

Extract of Beef.—Liebig's is useful in adding flavor to gravy or soup, and may be needed in case of illness.

Canned Fish.—Not so objectionable as canned meat, because preserved in oil. Salmon, sardines, mackerel, can be worked into palatable dishes for hasty meals now and then. Go light.

---

*For the process of jerking venison or beef, see my *Camping and Woodcraft*, p. 222. I have found that it succeeds even in the wet climate of the Southern Appalachians. (See also page 45.)

Smoked Fish.—Shredded codfish, for fish-balls, and smoked halibut, sprats, boneless herring, are portable and keep well. Enough for one or two meals of each may be relished.

Prepared Soups.—If liquid soups can be carried at all, take none but the very best brands that you can purchase. Concentrated (dry) soups, when of good quality, are a great help in time of trouble. Choose by trying samples before you leave home. They are kept by some camp outfitters, and by select groceries in the large cities. Erbswurst (a sort of pea-meal sausage used in the German army) is a pretty good emergency ration to carry when you hunt alone. Any good camp outfitter has it in stock or will order it for you.

Desiccated Eggs.—Baker's egg is a perfect substitute for fresh eggs in bake stuffs, and makes excellent omelets or scrambled eggs. A 1 lb. can, equal to about four dozen fresh eggs, measures 6x3x3 inches. It costs less than storage eggs, and the contents will never spoil if kept dry. The powder must soak about an hour in cold or lukewarm water before using. It may be put to soak overnight, or in a can or bottle of water when on the march. Thanks to this invention, the camp flapjack need no longer be a culinary horror.

I have tried other desiccated eggs, "made in Germany," which were uneatable by themselves, nor did they improve any dish that I tested them in.*

---

*On general principles I object to naming firms or brands; but when a good thing is not generally procurable in average stores, there would be no use in mentioning it without telling the reader where to get it. Out-of-town readers should get such catalogues as those of Montgomery Ward, Chicago; John Wanamaker, New York; Abercrombie & Fitch, New York.

Butter.—For ordinary trips it suffices to pack butter firmly into pry-up tin cans which have been sterilized by thorough scalding and then cooled in a perfectly clean place. Keep it in a spring or in cold running water (hung in a net, or weighted with a rock) whenever you can. When traveling, wrap the cold can in a towel or other insulating material.

Butter will keep fresh a long time if melted and gently boiled for a while, skimming off the scum as it rises, until the butter is as clear as oil, and then canning it. One-third less of this clarified butter equals the quantity of ordinary butter called for in any recipe.

Nut butter may be used as a substitute on bread.

Cheese.—According to taste, and only for occasional use. A small bottle of grated Parmesan for macaroni, etc.

Lard.—The amount will depend upon whether you use much lard in baking, and whether you fry with it or with bacon grease, oil, or butter. Olive oil is superior as a friture, especially for fish, but more expensive and more bothersome to carry.

Milk.—Sweetened condensed milk (the "salve" of the lumber jacks) is an abomination. The different brands of plain evaporated milk vary much in quality. Choose by actual test. The five cent cans are most convenient.

Two varieties of powdered milk (skimmed and whole, respectively) may be procured. The kind called "Trucream" makes four quarts of rich milk to the pound, by dissolving in water.

Potatoes.—If you can carry fresh ones, choose those with small eyes and of uniform medium size, even if you have to buy a bushel to sort out a peck.

Rice and grits are good substitutes when going light.

Onions.—A few fresh ones can be carried anywhere. Almost indispensable for seasoning soups, stews, etc.

Carrots.—A few of these, also, for soups and stews, if transportation permits.

Dehydrated (desiccated) Vegetables.—To my taste they are "rather poor fodder." On hard trips I prefer rice, grits, beans, and split peas.

Beans.—A prime factor in cold weather camping. Take a long time to cook ("soak all day and cook all night" is the rule). Cannot be cooked done at altitudes of five thousand feet and upward. Large varieties cook quickest, but the small white navy beans are best for baking. Pick them over before packing, as there is much waste.

Split Peas.—Used chiefly in making a thick, nourishing soup.

Canned Vegetables.—Very heavy and bulky for their fighting value. Very toothsome in the woods. Tomatoes are a good corrective of a meat diet. A few cans of baked beans (*without* tomato sauce) will be handy in bad weather. The three-quarter pound cans are convenient for emergency rations.

Canned Fruit.—Blackberries and pineapple go farthest. Cranberries for the bird season. Others are too watery.

Preserved Fruit.—The commissaries of the British army were wise when they gave jam an honorable place in Tommy Atkins' field ration. Yes: jam for soldiers in time of war. So many ounces of it, substituted, mind you, for so many ounces of the porky, porky, porky, that has ne'er a streak of lean. So, a little currant jelly with

your duck or venison is worth breaking all rules
for. Orange marmalade goes far. Such conserves
can be repacked by the buyer in pry-up cans that
have been sterilized as recommended under the
heading *Butter.*

Evaporated Fruit.—Dried apples and apricots
are best, owing to their tartness. Prunes are
rather bulky. Raisins go far, and are useful in
puddings. Dates help out an emergency ration,
and so do figs, which also are very good stewed or
in pudding.

Nuts.—Shelled nuts pay well for their transportation. Peanut butter is more easily digested,
and makes a good emergency food.

Sugar.—Granulated. Take plenty, especially if
you are short of other sweets. Men in the open
soon get to craving sweets, because sugar is stored-
up energy.

The "substitute" variously known as saccharin,
saxin, crystallose, is no substitute at all, save in
mere sweetening power, and even this has been
grossly exaggerated. The catalogues say "one
ounce equals in sweetening power one ton of sugar." The real ratio is one ounce to eighteen
pounds of sugar. This drug, which is derived
from coal tar, has decided medicinal qualities and
injures normal health if persistently taken. It
has none of the nutritive value of sugar.

Syrup.—A capital addition to pancakes, fried
mush, etc. Useful in cookery (baked beans, cakes,
etc.). Most maple syrup is adulterated. Be sure
of your brands.

Coffee.—The best coffee can only be made from
freshly roasted berries. Have it roasted and
ground the day before you start, and put up in

air-tight canisters. Take plenty; it will lose strength rapidly in the moist air of the woods.

Tea.—A much better pick-me-up than coffee or liquor, and more portable. English Breakfast suits most tastes.

Chocolate.—Very sustaining, as well as a good beverage. A quarter-pound cake carried in the pocket will pull a man through a hard day's wandering.

Acids.—The best way to carry vinegar is in one of the stone "pottles" that Holland gin comes in. If you carry pickles, let them be sour ones. Lemons are almost essential for hot-weather trips. A fair substitute is citric acid in crystals (any drugstore).

Condiments.—Salt is best carried in a wooden box. The amount used in cooking and at table is small, but if pelts are to be preserved or game shipped out, considerably more will be needed.

White pepper is better than black. Some cayenne or chili should also be taken.

Worcestershire sauce and tomato catchup (if genuine) are worth carrying when practicable; also mustard.

Pressed sage for stuffings, celery seed for soups, nutmeg and cloves (whole), perhaps ginger, cinnamon, and curry powder, will be needed.

Finally, a half pint of brandy, religiously reserved for brandy sauce, is worth its weight.

A ration list showing how much food of each kind is required, per man and per week, cannot be figured out satisfactorily unless one knows where the party is going, at what season of the year, how the stuff is to be carried, whether there is to be good chance of game or fish, and something about the men's personal tastes. However, the following table, based upon my own experience and allowing for many contingencies, may at least be useful as showing how to go about it.

The table gives four distinct estimates of food required by four men in two weeks, graded according as they travel light or heavy, in warm weather or in cold. The quantities will suffice without counting on game or fish. The difference between "light" and "heavy" is chiefly due to fresh potatoes and canned goods.

It will be noticed that the cold-weather ration that I give is more liberal than that for warm weather, and that the addition is mostly in fatty and oily foods. A man who eats little fat meat when living in the city will find that when he travels hard in cold weather and sleeps in the open air his system will demand more fatty food. The experience of travelers in the far North bears out the results of scientific analysis, that foods containing fats and oils are more nutritious and heat-producing than any others. But a steady diet of bread and bacon is likely to breed scurvy; so a supply of vegetables and fruits should be added. Men living in the open also develop a craving for sweets that is out of all proportion to what they experience in town. This is a normal demand, for sugar is stored-up energy. I have allowed liberally for this, and also for the increased consumption of coffee and tea that is the rule (owing somewhat to the fact that they lose strength from exposure to the air).

The table is chiefly valuable as showing the proper ratios of the meat, the bread, and the vegetable and fruit components. Under each of these headings the items can be varied a great deal, according to taste, but the aggregate of each component should be about as stated.

RATION LISTS, FOUR MEN, TWO WEEKS.
(56 RATIONS.)

Meats, etc.	LIGHT.		HEAVY.	
	Summer.	Winter.	Summer.	Winter.
Salt pork		10 lbs.		10 lbs.
Bacon	12 lbs.	12	10 lbs.	10
Ham	5	5	5	5
Dried beef or fish..	3	3	3	3
Canned meats			4	4
Canned fish			4	4
Beef extract	½	½	½	½
Concentrated soups.	2	2	2	2
Desiccated eggs....	2	2	2	2
Butter	6	6	6	6
Cheese			2	2
Lard	3	3	3	3
Powdered milk	3½	3½		
or Evaporated (28 small cans)			12½	12½
Lbs	37	47	54	64

Bread, etc.	LIGHT.		HEAVY.	
	Summer.	Winter.	Summer.	Winter.
Fresh bread			5 lbs.	5 lbs.
Wheat flour	24 lbs.	24 lbs.	20	20
Corn meal..........	5	10	5	10
Rice	5	5	5	5
Rolled oats	2	2	2	2
Grits	2	2	2	2
Macaroni	1	1	1	1
Baking powder	1½	1½	1	1
Lbs.	40½	45½	41	46

Vegetables.				
Potatoes (fresh)....			30 (½ bu.)	30
Onions (fresh)	5	5	5	5
Carrots (fresh)			5	5
Tomatoes (canned).		.	10 (4 cans)	10
Dehydrated vegetables	4	4		
Beans	4	6	4	6
Split peas	2	2	2	2
Canned baked beans.	3	3	3	3
Lbs.	18	20	59	61

Beverages.

Coffee (roasted, ground)	4	4	4	4
Tea	1	1	1	1
Chocolate (unsweetened)	1	1	1	1
Lbs.	6	6	6	6

	LIGHT.		HEAVY.	
Sweets.	Summer.	Winter.	Summer.	Winter.
Sugar (granulated).	8	10	5	5
Syrup			3 (1 qt.)	6
Jelly, jam, marmalade			5	5
Lbs.	8	10	13	16

Acids.

Vinegar			1 (pint)	1
Pickles			2	2
Lemons			4 (2 doz.)	
Citric acid (c. p., cryst.)	¼	¼		
Lbs.	¼	¼	7	8

Fruits, etc.

Evaporated apples, apricots	3	3	3	3
Raisins, dates, figs..	2	2	2	2
Canned blackberries, cranberries, pineapple			24 (12 cans)	24
Shelled nuts, or nut butter	2	2	2	2
Lbs.	7	7	31	31

Condiments.

Salt (if allowing for curing skins, etc., take 10 lbs.)	2	2	2	2
Pepper (white)....	1 oz.	1 oz.	1 oz.	1 oz.
Cayenne or chili...	1 oz.	1 oz.	1 oz.	1 oz.
Worcestershire sauce.			1 bot.	1 bot.
Olive oil			1 bot.	1 bot.
Tomato catchup			1 bot.	1 bot.
Brandy			½ pint.	½ pint.
Mustard			1 bot.	1 bot.
Sage, celery seed, nutmeg, cloves, cinnamon, ginger, curry powder ...	x	x	x	x
Lbs.	2¼	2¼	6	6

	LIGHT.		HEAVY.	
	Summer.	Winter.	Summer.	Winter.
Total lbs.	119	138	217	233
Per man, per day	2⅛	2½	3⅞	4⅛

Meat of any kind will quickly mould or spoil if packed in tins from which air is not exhausted. Put pork, bacon, or ham in loose cheesecloth bags that can be hung up in camp, and pack them in parchment paper for transit; so also cheese. Flour, meal, cereals, vegetables, and dried fruits go in stout bags. Ordinary flour sacks are too weak, and wet through too easily. Salt, as it draws moisture, is best carried in a wooden box or screw-top wooden mailing tubes; butter, coffee, tea, sugar, jam, etc., in pry-up tin cans. Camp outfitters supply small bags and tins of various sizes that stow in waterproof provision bags, and it saves trouble to buy them ready-made. Label everything plainly.

One of the handiest things in a camper's kit is surgeon's rubber adhesive plaster. This can be purchased at any drugstore. A ten-yard spool

each of the one-inch and two-inch widths will
be useful in a hundred ways. This plaster is
waterproof and air-tight. It will stick to any dry
surface (wood, metal, glass, cloth, leather, or
skin), and will stay there until purposely removed; yet it can be peeled off and reapplied
many times. As an instantaneous mender of
rents and stopper of holes or cracks it has no
equal.

One of the most bothersome things in shifting
camp is to secure opened cans and bottles from
spilling. Surgeon's plaster does the trick in a
twinkling. Put a little square of it over each
hole in the milk can that you opened for breakfast, and there will be no leakage. To hold a
cork in a bottle, stick a narrow strip of the plaster
over the cork and down opposite sides of the bottle's neck. To protect the bottle from breaking,
run a strip around it at top and one at bottom.

The caps of baking powder cans or similar
tins can be secured to the bodies in the same way.
With a broad strip you can seal a box or chest
water-tight, stop a leak in a canoe, or mend a
broken rod, a paddle, a gunstock, or even an axe-
handle (first nailing it). A chest or cupboard can
be extemporized from any packing box, in a jiffy,
by cleating the top and using surgeon's plaster for
hinges.

Camp chests are very convenient when it is
practicable to carry them; but they should be
small, weighing not over fifty or sixty pounds each
when packed, so that one man can easily handle
them unassisted. If they are specially made, cottonwood is the best material (if thoroughly seasoned boards can be had—otherwise it warps
abominably). It is the strongest and toughest

wood for its weight that we have, and will not splinter. For the ends and lids of small chests, ⅝-inch stuff is thick enough, and ⅜-inch for the sides, bottoms, and trays. The bottom should have a pair of ⅝-inch cleats for risers and the top a similar pair to keep it from warping, unless the chests are to go on pack animals. Strap-hinges and hasp, a brass padlock and broad leather end-straps (not drop-handles) should be provided, and the chest painted.

The best size is 24x18x9 inches, this being convenient for canoes and pack-saddles. A pine grocery box of this size, with ¾-inch ends and ⅜-inch sides, top, and bottom, weighs only 10 pounds, and will answer the purpose very well. Screw a wooden handle on each end, say 5x2 inches, with a hand-hold gouged out of the under side.

Check off every article in the outfit as it is stowed, and keep the inventory for future reference. Then note what is left over at the end of the trip. This will help in outfitting for the next season.

CHAPTER II.

UTENSILS.

A PARTY going into fixed camp, within wagon call of the railroad, can carry a sheet-steel stove. A good pattern is the Klondike stove shown in the illustration. Its best feature is the size of the fire-box, which takes in wood twenty-eight inches long and thick enough to keep an all-night fire, the stove being closed air-tight. The top of the Klondike, 14x30 inches, is free for utensils; the oven, above it, takes a 10x14 pan for baking or roasting. Oven, legs, and pipe stow inside the body of the stove, leaving space for a 12x13x9½-inch galvanized box that holds cooking utensils for four persons and can be used in camp as a dish-pan or as a vermin-proof box for provisions. When packed for transportation, the stove measures 30x14x12 inches, and weighs 29 pounds (complete with box and utensils, 43½ pounds).

In rough country, especially if camp is to be shifted frequently, a stove is out of the reckoning. If pack animals are taken, or the trip is by canoe, without long and difficult portages, it pays to take along either a folding grate or a pair of fire irons. Various patterns of grates are shown in outfitters' catalogues. I have used one called the Gem which is satisfactory of its kind. It weighs 3¼ pounds, is 16x28 inches when set up, and folds into a package 1½x19 inches.

A lighter grate is Sackett's camp broiler, 9x14 inches. The legs do not lock in place, and hence are of little use on stony or mushy ground. I remove them, and so have a good grate and broiler weighing only one pound, yet big enough to support a frying pan and coffee pot when laid across a couple of logs or rocks.

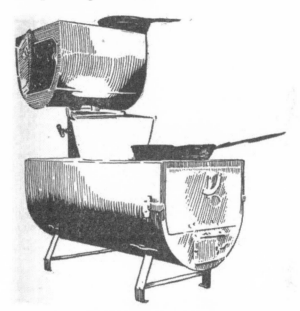

KLONDIKE CAMP STOVE.

Fire "irons" are simply two pieces of flat steel 24x1½x⅛ inches, weighing 2½ pounds, which are used like the broiler named above. If a mule steps on one of them, it (mule or iron) can quickly be hammered back into correct form.

On light marching trips no support for the utensils will be carried. Rocks or logs will take their place.   There may be a little more spilling and swearing, but less tired backs.

It is commonly agreed that four is the ideal number for a camping party, at least among hunters and fishermen.   Certainly no larger number should attempt their own cooking.   Utensils and table ware for such a party, going light, should include: a large frying-pan (more serviceable than two small ones); a pan to mix dough in and wash dishes (common milk pan); a stout, seamless, covered pot for boiling or stewing meat, baking beans,

SACKETT'S BROILER.

etc.; a medium pot or pail for hot water (always wanted, substitute for tea kettle); a smaller one for cereals, vegetables, fruit; and either a coffee pot low enough to nest in the latter, or a covered pail in its place.   There should be six plates (two for serving) and four each of cups, knives, forks, teaspoons, tablespoons.   This is about as little as the party can well get along with.

It will be bothersome to bake bread for four in the frying-pan.   Add a reflector or common sheet-

steel "roaster and baker," if practicable. A wire
broiler, a tea percolator, and a corkscrew and can
opener will nest with this set. If the cook wears
no sheath knife a butcher knife is essential. Two
dish towels (one to be divided into clouts) and
a couple of yards of cheesecloth for straining and
to hang meat in should be taken.

The common utensils of the shops will not nest.
They are all spouts and handles, bail ears and
cover knobs. Still, a good deal can be done by
substitution. Covered pails do all the work of
sauce pans and kettles, and are better all round,
for they can either be set upon the coals or hung
above the fire; besides, you can carry water in

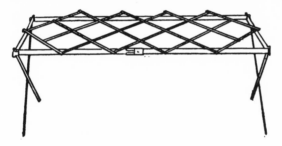

GEM FOLDING GRATE.

them, and their covers keep heat in and ashes
out. All such vessels should be low and broad;
then they will boil quickly and pack well. Good
proportions are:

3 quarts....diameter 6¾ in. x 5¼ in. height.
4   "   ....   "   7½ " x 5¾ "   "
6   "   ....   "   8½ " x 6½ "   "
8   "   ....   "   9¼ " x 7½ "   "

Bail ears should project as little as possible. Lids should have fold-down rings instead of knobs. If the bails interfere with nesting, substitute light chains.

Ordinary coffee pots are too tall and slender. The best form is what is known as a coffee boiler (see illustration), which nests inside a comparatively small pail, boils quickly, has a bail,

COOKING KIT FOR SIX.

Nesting in space 11 x 12⅞ inches, and weighing 17¼ lbs.

and is fitted with a solid spout that will not melt off. A similar article of tin is known as a "miner's coffee pot." When compact nesting is aimed at, discard the coffee pot in favor of a lidded pail. It has the advantage that no aroma escapes through a spout. Use a percolator of aluminum (cylindrical, not egg-shaped) that is large enough for both coffee and tea, and remove its wings.

Tin cups that nest inside the coffee pot have the lower part of the handle free. Get the 1½-pint size (5x2⅛ in.). Small cups and small plates are a nuisance in camp. Tin is not nice to drink hot fluids from: it makes tea "taste." Aluminum is worse, for it blisters the unwary mouth. I

carry my own cup at my belt or in my pouch, for
it is wanted ten times a day. It is of white enameled ware. If every man does this, there will be
no trouble about cups nesting.

Plates, too, should be of enameled ware, for it
is so much easier to clean than tin or aluminum.
Let them be deep and generous (9½-inch soup
plates, nesting in the frying pan).

The frying-pan handle is a perennial problem.
The best form of detachable handle that I know
of is Darling's. A stick can be inserted in it, for
long-distance frying, by those who do not know
that frying should never be done over a fierce fire,
nor that a few coals raked to one side do the trick.

Few camp cooking kits include a baker, although it is almost essential for comfortable life
in the woods. The most portable form is the folding reflector sold by most outfitters. It is similar
to those that our great-grandmothers used to bake
biscuit in, before a hearth fire. The top slants
like a shed roof, and the bottom like another shed
roof turned upside down, the bread pan being in
the middle. The slanting top and bottom reflect
heat downward upon the top of the baking and
upward against its bottom, so that bread, for instance, bakes evenly all around.

A prime advantage of this cunning utensil is
that baking can proceed immediately when the fire
is kindled, without waiting for the wood to burn
down to coals, and without danger of burning the
dough. Fish, flesh, and fowl can be roasted to a
turn in this contrivance. It has several better
points than an oven, chief of which is its porta-
bility, as it folds flat; but it is inferior for corn
bread, army bread, etc., and impossible for pot-
roasts or braising.

The best size of reflector for two men is 12x 12x8 inches, the pan of which holds just a dozen biscuits. For four men, a good size is 16x18x8. These sizes are the height, width, and depth, respectively, when the oven is open for use. When folded it is only about an inch thick. The 8x12 size weighs 2 pounds, with bake pan; the 8x18 size, 2¾ pounds. A canvas carrying case, which is needed, for the baker is frail, adds another pound. A wire broiler packs inside the reflector; it is not necessary for broiling meat, but it is handy for the purpose, and especially for broiling fish.

The old-fashioned Dutch oven of cast iron is too heavy for any but wagon parties, and by them is usually discarded for a camp stove.

A much cheaper utensil than the reflector, and one that can be used like a Dutch oven, with coals underneath and on top, is the sheet-steel baker or roaster designed for use in stove ovens. With the two sections nesting, it is quite portable. The 15x10x7 size weighs, with bake pan, about 4¼ pounds.

A good-sized water pail is a great convenience in camp. The best form of all is a galvanized pail with bail ears set below the rim and a tight cover fitting *outside* the top. It is strong enough to go on a pack saddle, and is an excellent container for perishables. In a canoe it is much 'handier and more reliable than the japanned bread box so often used as a provision chest. With a broad strip of surgeon's plaster around the rim it is perfectly water-tight and the cover cannot come off. Don't be bluffed by its name: it is called a garbage can.

Men who have neither time nor inclination to

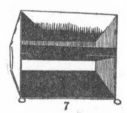

1. Coffee Boiler.
2. Miner's Coffee Pot.
3. Percolator.
4. Miner's Cup,

5. Baker.
6. Water Bucket.
7. Reflector.
8. Frying Pan.

rummage the stores for "calamities" that will nest would do well to pay extra for outfits already kitted by camp outfitters. Using one outfitter's sets for illustration, we are offered:

Set for.	*Size, nested.*	*In "Armorsteel."*		*In "Aluminol."*	
Two persons ...	9½ x 8¾ in.	6¾ lbs.	$4.00	6⅝ lbs.	$9.85
Four persons ...	10 x 11¼ in.	12 lbs.	6.25	10⅞ lbs.	16.60
Six persons	11 x 12⅞ in.	17½ lbs.	8.50	17¼ lbs.	26.50
Eight persons ..	11 x 12⅞ in.	19¼ lbs.	9.40	18¾ lbs.	30.00

In the four-men and eight-men sets the coffee pots will be found rather stingy. An 8x18 folding reflector, broiler, canvas case, butcher knife, cooking spoon, and percolator would add exactly 4 pounds weight and $6.40 to the price.

"Aluminol" is an aluminum alloy that is tougher and more durable than the common aluminum of the shops. The latter is too soft and too easily bent or dented, and it will not stand dry heat. Aluminum frying pans are worthless: food sticks to them and burns.

"Armorsteel" utensils are made from strong steel stamped in one solid piece, and doubly tinned.

Ordinary tinware is much lighter and cheaper than either of these, but here its merits end. It will not stand rough handling; rusts easily, is hard to clean when greasy, and its soldered joints are always treacherous.

Enameled ware is the easiest of all to keep clean. It is the best material to cook fruit in. Its tendency to chip and flake in cold weather can be tamed by warming gradually, at such times, before exposing to fierce heat. It is not much heavier than any other ware that is strong enough for outdoor service.

Men who must travel with very light equipment should cut out all but the absolutely essential utensils, and have them strong enough for hard service.   Ideal   outfitting   is   to   have   what   we want, when we want it, and *never to be bothered with anything else.*

CHAPTER III.

FIRES.

THE success of outdoor cookery depends largely upon how the fire is built and how it is managed. A camper is known by his fire. It is quite impossible to prepare a good meal over a higgledy-piggledy heap of smoking chunks, a fierce blaze, or a great bed of coals that will warp iron and melt everything else.

For a noonday lunch, or any other quick meal, when you have only to boil coffee and fry something, a large fire is not wanted. Drive a forked stake in the ground, lay a green stick across it, slanting upward from the ground, and weight the lower end with a rock or peg it down with an inverted crotch. The slanting stick should have the stub of a twig left at its upper end to hold the pot bail in place, and should be set at such an angle that the pot swings about two feet clear of the ground.

Then gather a small armful of sound, dry twigs from the size of a lead pencil to that of your finger. Take no twig that lies flat on the ground, for such are generally damp or rotten. Choose hardwood, if there is any, for it lasts well.

Select three of your best sticks for kindling. Shave each of them almost through, for half its length, leaving lower end of shavings attached to the stick, one under the other. Stand these in a tripod, under the hanging pot, with their curls down. Around them build a conical wigwam of the other sticks, standing each on end and slanting to a common center. Leave free air spaces between the sticks. Fire requires air, and plenty of it, and it burns best when it has something to climb up on; hence the wigwam construction. Now touch off the shaved sticks, and in a moment you will have a small blast furnace under the pot. This will get up steam in a hurry.

Meantime get two bed-sticks, five or six inches thick, to support the frying pan. The firewood will all drop to embers soon after the pot boils. Toss out the smoking butts, leaving only clear, glowing coals. Put your bed-sticks on either side, parallel and level. Set the pan on them, and fry away. So, in fifteen or twenty minutes from the time you drove your stake, the meal will be cooked.

A man acting without system or forethought, in even so simple a matter as this, can waste an hour in pottering over smoky mulch, or blistering himself before a bonfire, and it will be an ill mess of half-burned stuff that he serves in the end.

When making a "one-night stand," start a small cooking fire the moment you stop for camping and put your kettle on. Then you will have coals and boiling water ready when you begin cooking, and the rest is easy.

For baking in a reflector, or roasting a joint, a high fire is best, with a backing to throw the heat forward. Sticks three feet long can be leaned against a big log or a sheer-faced rock, and the kindling started under them.

Often a good bed of coals is wanted. The

camp-fire generally supplies these, but sometimes
they are needed in a hurry, soon after camp is
pitched. To get them, take *sound hardwood,*
either green or dead, and split it into sticks of
uniform thickness (say 1¼-inch face). Lay down
two bed-sticks, cross these near the ends with two
others, and so on up until you have a pen a foot
high. Start a fire in this pen. Then cover it with
a layer of parallel sticks laid an inch apart. Cross
this with a similar layer at right angles, and so
upward for another foot. The free draft will
make a roaring fire, and all will burn down to
coals together. The thick bark of hemlock, and
of hardwoods generally, will soon yield coals for
ordinary cooking.

To keep coals a long time, cover them with
ashes, or with bark which will soon burn to ashes.
In wet weather a bed of coals can be shielded by
slanting broad strips of green bark over it and
overlapping them at the edges. In windy weather
build your fire in a trench.

Camp-fires, as distinguished from cooking-fires,
are usually built by laying down two short, thick
logs five or six feet apart, for bed-sticks, crossing
these with two parallel logs about a foot apart,
and firing with small poles between them. Such a
fire is generally too hot for good cooking, and it
blazes or smokes too much. Cook in front of it,
or to one side, with coals raked from under the
forestick.

When staying several days in one place, build
a separate cooking-fire. It saves trouble in the
end. On a level spot near the camp-fire set up
two stout forked stakes about five feet apart and
four feet to the crotches. Across them lay a green
stick (lug-pole) somewhat thicker than a broom-

stick. Now cut three or four green crotches from branches, drive a nail in the small end of each, invert the crotches, and hang them on the lug-pole to suspend kettles from. These pot-hooks are to be of different lengths so that the kettle can be adjusted to different heights above the fire, first for hard boiling, and then for simmering. If kettles were hung from the lug-pole itself, this adjustment could not be made, and you would have to dismount the whole business in order to get one kettle off.

Then get two thick, flat rocks and bed them under the lug-pole to support your fire-irons or the frying pan itself. A pair of green logs will do if there are no rocks handy.

There is much in knowing how to select fuel. As a rule, hardwoods make good, slow-burning fuel that produces lasting coals, while softwoods make a quick, hot fire that soon dies to useless ashes.

The following woods will scarcely burn at all when they are green: aspen (large-toothed), black ash, balsam, box elder, buckeye, hemlock, pitch pine, sassafras, sourwood, sycamore, tamarack, tupelo (sour gum), water oak, poplar (tulip), and service berry. Butternut, chestnut, red oak, red maple, and persimmon burn very slowly in a green state.• Such woods are good for backlogs, hand-junks, or andirons, and for side-logs in a cooking-fire that is to be used continuously. Yellow birch and white ash, on the contrary, are better for a camp-fire when green than when they are seasoned. It may be said, in general, that green wood burns best in winter, when the sap is down. Trees that grow on high, dry ground burn better than those of the same species that stand in moist soil. Chestnut cut on the summits of the southern Appalachians burns freely, even when green, and the mountain beech burns as ardently as birch.

Arbor-vitæ (Northern "white cedar") and chestnut burn to dead coals that do not communicate flame. They, as well as box elder, red cedar, hemlock, sassafras, tulip, balsam, tamarack, and spruce, make a great crackling and snapping in the fire. All of the soft pines, too, are prone to pop. Certain hardwoods, such as sugar maple, beech, white oak, and sometimes hickory, must be watched for a time after the fire is started, because the embers that they shoot out are long-lived, and hence more dangerous than those of softwoods; but they are splendid fuel, for all that.

The following woods are very hard to split: Blue ash, box elder, buckeye, cherry, white elm, winged elm, sour gum, hemlock (generally), liquidambar (sweet gum), honey locust, sugar maple, sycamore, tupelo. Some woods, however, that are stubborn when seasoned are readily split when green, such as hickory, beech, dogwood, sugar maple, birch, and slippery elm.

Firewoods that split easily are: Hackberry, red oak, basket oak, white oak, ash, and white birch.

Best of all Northern firewoods is hickory, green or dry. It makes a hot fire, but lasts a long time, burning down to a bed of hard coals that keep up an even, generous heat for hours. Hickory, by the way, is distinctly an American tree; no other region on earth produces it. The live oak of the South is most excellent fuel. Following the hickory, in fuel value, are the chestnut oak, overcup, post and basket oaks, pecan, the hornbeams (ironwoods), and dogwood. The latter burns finally to a beautiful white ash that is characteristic; apple wood does the same. Black birch also ranks here; it has the advantage of "doing its own blowing," as a Carolina mountaineer said to me, meaning that the oil in the birch assists its combustion so that the wood needs no coaxing. All of the birches are good fuel, ranking in about this order: black, yellow, red, paper, and white. Sugar maple was the favorite fuel of our old-time hunters and surveyors, because it ignites easily, burns with a clear, steady flame, and leaves good coals.

Locust is a good, lasting fuel; it is easy to cut, and, when green, splits fairly well; the thick bark takes fire readily, and the wood then burns slowly, with little flame, leaving pretty good coals; hence it is good for night-wood. Mulberry has similar qualities. The best of the oaks for fuel, especially when green, is white oak; it also splits very readily. The scarlet and willow oaks are among the poorest of the hardwoods for fuel. Cherry makes only fair fuel. White elm is poor stuff, but slippery elm is better.

In some respects white ash is the best of green woods for campers' fuel. It is easily cut and split, is lighter to tote than most other hardwoods, and is of so dry a nature that even the green wood catches fire readily. It burns with clear flame, and lasts longer than any other free-burning wood of its weight.

Most of the softwoods are good only for kindling, or for quick cooking-fires. Liquidambar, magnolia, poplar (tulip), catalpa, red cedar, and willow are poor fuel. Seasoned chestnut and poplar make a hot fire, but crackle and leave no coals. Balsam fir, basswood, and the white and

loblolly pines make quick fires but are soon spent.
The gray (Labrador) pine is considered good fuel
in the far North, where hardwoods are scarce.
Seasoned tamarack is fairly good. Spruce is poor
fuel, although, being resinous, it kindles easily and
makes a good blaze for "branding up" a fire.
Pitch pine, which is the most inflammable of all
woods when dry and "fat," will scarcely burn
at all in a green state. Sycamore and buckeye,
when thoroughly seasoned, are good fuel, but will
not split. Alder burns readily and gives out considerable heat, but is not lasting. The wood of
the large-toothed aspen will not burn when green,
yet when dry it burns freely, does not crackle,
lasts well, and leaves good coals. The best green
softwoods for fuel are white birch, paper birch,
soft maple, cottonwood, and quaking aspen.

As a rule, the timber growing along the mar-
gins of large streams is softwood. Hence drift-
wood is generally a poor mainstay, unless there
is plenty of it on the spot.

The best kindling is fat pine, or the bark of the
paper birch. Fat pine is found in the stumps and
butt cuts of pine trees that died on the stump.
The resin has collected there and dried. This
wood is usually easy to split. Pine knots are
the tough, heavy, resinous stubs of limbs that
are found on dead pine trees. They, as well as
fat pine, are almost imperishable, and those sticking out of old rotten logs are as good as any.
The knots of balsam fir are similarly used. Hemlock knots are worthless and will ruin an axe.
The thick bark of hemlock, and of hardwoods
generally, is good to make glowing coals in a
hurry.

In a hardwood forest the best kindling, sure to

be dry underneath the bark in all weathers, is procured by snapping off the small dead branches, or stubs of branches, that are left on the trunks of medium-sized trees. Do not pick up twigs from the ground, but choose those, among the downwood, that are held up free from the ground. Where a tree is found that has been shivered by lightning, or one that has broken off without uprooting, good splinters of dry wood will be found. In every laurel thicket there is plenty of dead laurel, and, since it is of sprangling growth, most of the branches will be free from the ground and snap-dry. They ignite readily and give out intense heat.

It is a good test of one's resourcefulness to make a fire out of doors in rainy weather. The best way to go about it depends upon local conditions. Dry fuel and a place to build the fire can often be found under big uptilted logs, shelving rocks, and similar natural shelters, or in the core of an old stump. In default of these, look for a dead softwood tree that leans to the south. The wood and bark on the under side will be dry —chop some off, split it fine, and build your fire under the shelter of the trunk.

To light a match in the wind, *face* the wind. Cup your hands, with their backs toward the wind, and hold the match with its head pointing toward the rear of the cup—*i. e.*, toward the wind. Remove the right hand just long enough to strike the match on something very close by; then instantly resume the former position. The flame will run up the match stick, instead of being blown away from it, and so will have something to feed on.

Never leave a fire, or even a spark, behind you. Put it out.

CHAPTER IV.

DRESSING AND KEEPING GAME AND FISH.

IT is not necessary to hang a deer up to skin and butcher it; but that is the more cleanly way. One man, unassisted, can hang a pretty heavy animal in the following way: Drag it headforemost to a sapling that is just limber enough to bend near the ground when you climb it. Cut three poles, ten or twelve feet long, with crotches near the ends. Climb the sapling and trim off the top, leaving the stub of one stout branch near the top. Tie your belt into a loop around the deer's antlers or throat. Bend the sapling down until you can slip the loop over the end of the sapling. The latter, acting as a spring-pole, will lift part of the deer's weight. Then place the crotches of the poles under the fork of the sapling, the butts of the poles radiating outward, thus forming a tripod. Push first on one pole, then on another, and so raise the carcass free from the ground.

If you do not intend to butcher the deer immediately, raise it up out of reach of roving dogs and "varmints," and put a smudge under it of rotten wood, well banked with stones and earth so that it cannot blow around and set the woods afire. The smudge will help to keep away blow-flies and birds of prey, and will guide you back to the place.

36

It is common practice to hang deer by gambrels
with the head down; but, when hung head up, the
animal is easier to skin, easier to butcher, drains
better, and does not drip blood and juices over
the neck and head, which you may want to have
mounted for a trophy. Dried blood is very hard
to remove from hair or fur. If the skin is
stripped off from rear to head it will be hard to
grain.

The more common way of skinning a deer, when
the head is not wanted for mounting, is to hang it
up by one hind leg and begin skinning at the
hock, peeling the legs, then the body, and finally
the neck, then removing the head with skin on
(for baking in a hole), after which the carcass is
swung by both legs and is eviscerated.

If this is a buck, you may wish to save the head
for mounting. For this, the skin of the whole
neck must be preserved, clear back to the shoul-
ders. Cleanse away any blood that may have is-
sued from the nose and mouth and stuff some dry
moss, or other absorbent, in the beast's mouth.
Open your jackknife, insert the point, edge up,
where the neck joins the back, and cut the skin
in a circle around the base of the neck, running
from the withers down over the front of the shoul-
der-blade to the brisket or point of the breast on
each side. Do not skin the head at present—
you may not have time for that. Insert the point
of the knife through the skin over the paunch, and,
following the middle line of the chest, slit upward
to meet the cut around the neck. Then reverse,
and continue the slit backward to the end of the
tail, being careful not to perforate the walls of
the belly. Then slit along the inside of each leg
from the hoof to the belly-slit. If you wish to

save the feet for mounting, be particular to rip the
skin in a straight line up the *under* side of the leg,
starting by inserting the point of the knife between the heel-pads.

Now comes a nice trick, that of severing the
shanks. Nearly every in-
experienced person starts
too high. Study the ac-
companying illustrations of
these joints, noting where
the arrow points, which is
the place to use your knife.
In a deer the joint is about
an inch and a half below
the hock on the hind leg,
and an inch below the knee
on the fore leg. Cut square across through
skin and muscles, in front, and similarly behind;
then, with a quick pull backward against your
knee, snap the shank off. The joint of the fore
leg is broken in a similar manner, excepting that
it is snapped forward.

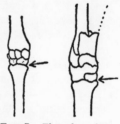

Fig. 7.—The place to
Use Your Knife.

From *Forest and Stream.*

Having stripped the vertebræ from the tail, now
peel the skin off the whole animal, from the shoul-
ders downward, assisting with your closed fist,
and, where necessary, with the knife; but wherever the knife is used be careful to scrape the
skin as clean as you can, without cutting it, for
every adhering bit of fat, flesh, or membrane must
be thoroughly removed before the skin is ready
for tanning, and that is easier to do now than
after it dries. The whole operation of skinning
is much easier while the animal is still warm than
after the body has become cold. To skin a frozen
animal is a desperately mean job. I have known

four old hunters to work nearly a whole after-
noon in skinning a frozen bear.

The skin of the body and limbs having been removed, stretch it out flat, hair side down, alongside of you to receive portions of the meat as it is
butchered. Now take up your knife, insert its
point alongside the breastbone, and cut through
the false ribs to the point of the sternum. In a
young animal this is easy; but in an old one the
ribs have ossified, and you must search for the
soft points of union between the ribs and the sternum, which are rather hard to find. Here your
knife's temper, and perhaps your own, will be put
to the test. The most trifling-looking pocket
hatchet would do the trick in a jiffy.

Open the abdominal cavity, taking care not to
rupture anything, and prop the chest open a few
inches with a stick, or by merely pulling the ribs
away from each other. Cut the diaphragm free
at both sides and at the back. (It is the membrane that separates the organs of the chest from
those of the abdomen.) Everything now is free
from the body except at the throat and anus.
Reach in and take in your grasp all the vessels that
run up into the neck. With knife in the other
hand, cut them across from above downward, taking care that you do not cut yourself. Now pull
away gradually, helping a little here and there
with the knife until all the contents of the visceral
cavity lie at your feet, save the lower end of the
rectum, which is still attached. With a hatchet,
if you had one, you would now split the pelvis.
The thing can be done with a large knife, if the
animal is not too old, by finding the soft suture at
the highest part of the bone and rocking the knife-
edge on it. But you may not be able to accom-

plish this just now. So reach in with the jack-knife, cut carefully around the rectum and urinary organs, keeping as close to the bone as possible, and free everything from the cavity. If water is near, wash out the abdominal cavity and let it drain.

To remove the head; flay back the skin for several inches at base of neck, cut through flesh, etc., to the backbone. Search along this till you find the flat joint between the faces of two vertebræ, separate these as far as you can; then twist the attached part of the body round and round, until it breaks off.*

In butchering, save the liver, heart, brain, milt (spleen), kidneys, and the caul fat. The caul is the fold of membrane loaded with fat that covers most of the intestines. In removing the liver you need not bother about a gall-bladder, for a deer has none. Many a tenderfoot has been tricked into looking for it.

If one is in a hurry, and is not particular about the hide, he can do his butchering on the ground. In that case, lay the animal on sloping ground, with its head uphill; or bend its back over a log or rock; or turn it on its back with its head twisted around and wedged under one side.

In butchering an elk or moose that has antlers, first remove the head. Then turn the body on its back and prop it in position with a couple of three-foot stakes sharpened at both ends, a hole being dug for a moose's withers. Sometimes only the haunches, sirloins, and tongue are saved, these being cut away without skinning or gutting the carcass.

---

*Directions how to skin a head for mounting are given in my *Camping and Woodcraft*, Chap. XIX.

Bears are skinned on the ground, beginning the incisions at the feet and leaving the scalp, or skin of the whole head, attached. It is quite a task to flesh the pelts, as they are fatty and greasy. All of the caul fat should be saved for rendering into bear's oil, which is much better and wholesomer than lard. The brain, liver, and milt are good eating.

If a hide is to be preserved for some time in a green state, use nothing on it but salt. Spread it out flat, hair side down, stretch the legs, flanks, etc., and rub all parts thoroughly with salt, particular pains being taken to leave no little fold untreated. A moose-hide will take ten or even fifteen pounds of salt. As soon as the salting is done, fold in the legs and roll the hide up.

When a deer has merely been eviscerated and is hung up to be skinned, and cut up at a more convenient season, prop open the abdominal cavity with a stick, so that it may dry out quickly. If the weather is warm enough at any hour of the day for flies to come out, keep a smudge going under the carcass. It takes flies but a few minutes to raise Ned with venison. If blows are discovered on the meat, remove them, looking especially at all folds and nicks in the meat, and around the bones, for the blows work into such places very quickly. So long as they have not bored into the flesh they do it no harm.

It may be said here that even smoked bacon is not immune from blows, and it should not be hung up without a cheesecloth cover. The fly that blows meats is the same that starts "skippers" in cheese.

Hornaday gives the following rule, in his *Natural History,* for computing the live weight of

deer from the dressed weight: Add four ciphers
to the dressed weight in pounds, and divide by
78,612; the quotient will be the live weight in
pounds.

Now for what Shakespeare calls "small deer":
I must take issue with Nessmuk on the art of
skinning a squirrel. He says: "Chop off head,
tail, and feet with the hatchet; cut the skin on
the back crosswise, and, inserting the two middle
fingers, pull the skin off in two parts (head and
tail). Clean and cut the squirrel in halves, leaving two ribs on the hind quarters." The objec-
tion is that, in this case, you throw away the best
part of the squirrel, the cheek meat and brain
being its special tid-bits.

A better way is this: Sever the tail from below, holding your left forefinger close in behind
it, and cutting through the vertebræ close up to
the body, leaving only the hide on the top side.
Then turn the squirrel over and cut a slit down
along each ham. Put your foot on the tail, hold
the rear end of the squirrel in your hand, and pull,
stripping the skin off to the fore legs. Peel the
skin from the hind legs, and cut off the feet. Then
cut off the fore feet. Skin to the neck; assist here
a little with the knife; then skin to the ears; cut
off the butts of the ears; then skin till the blue
of the eyeballs shows, and cut; then to the nose till
the teeth show, and cut it off. Thus you get no
hair on the meat, and the whole thing is done in
less than a minute.

Turkeys, geese, ducks, and grouse are usually
dry picked. If this could be done while the
bodies were still warm, it would be no job at all;
but after they are cold it generally results in a
good deal of laceration of the skin—so much so

that sometimes the disgusted operator gives up and skins the whole bird. It would be better to scald them first, like chickens. In dry picking, hang the bird up by one leg, pluck first the pinions and tail feathers; then the small feathers from shanks and inside of thighs; then the others. Grasp only a few feathers at a time between finger and thumb, as close to the skin as possible, and pull quickly toward the head. Then pick out all pin-feathers and quills. Singe the down off quickly, so as not to give an oily appearance to the skin. Ordinarily the down can be removed from a duck's breast by grasping the bird by the neck and giving one sweep of the open hand down one side of the body and then one down the other. In plucking geese or ducks some use finely powdered resin to remove the pin-feathers. The bird is plucked dry, then rubbed all over with the resin, dipped in and out of boiling water seven or eight times, and then the pin-feathers and down are easily rubbed off.

To draw a bird: cut off the head, and the legs at the first joint. Make a lengthwise slit on back at base of neck and sever neck bone close to body, also the membrane which holds the windpipe. Make a lengthwise incision from breastbone to (and around) the vent, so you can easily draw the insides, which must be done carefully, so as not to rupture the gall-bladder. The idea that ducks and other game birds should hang until they smell badly is monstrous. If you want to know where such tastes originated, read the annals of medieval sieges.

A small trout is easily cleaned by tearing out the gills with thumb and forefinger and drawing the inside out with them. In a large trout the gills should be cut free from the lower jaw and back of head, and a slit cut along the under side from head to fin; the inside is then drawn out by the gills, leaving the fish clean within.

To scale a fish: grasp it by the head, and, using a knife that is not over-keen, scale first one side and then the other, with swift, steady sweeps toward you. The scales below the gills, and those near the fins, are removed by moving the point of the knife crosswise to the fish's length. Next place the knife just below the belly fin and with a slant stroke cut off this, the side fins, and the head, all in one piece. Then remove the back fin, and the spines beneath it, by making a deep incision on each side of the fin and pulling the latter out. The ventral part is removed in the same way. Open the fish, wash it in cold water, scrape off the slime, and then wipe it *dry* with a clean cloth or towel. Large fish, for broiling, should be split open along the back and the spine removed.

Some fish, such as yellow perch, are better skinned than scaled. Grasp the fish firmly, belly down. Cut across the nape of the neck, run the point of the knife along the back to the tail, and on each side of the back fin. Remove the fin by catching lower end between thumb and knife blade and pulling smartly upward toward the head. Skin each side by seizing between thumb and knife the flap of skin at nape and jerking outward and downward; then the rest, by grasping skin as near the vent as possible and tearing quickly down to the tail, bring away the anal fin. Remove the head and the entrails will come with it. Trout and pickerel should be scraped free of slime.

To skin a bullhead: cut off the ends of the

spines, slit the skin behind and around the head, and then from this point along the back to the tail, cutting around the back fin. Then peel the two corners of the skin well down, sever the backbone, and, holding to the corners of the skin with one hand, pull the fish's body free from the skin with the other.

To skin an eel: nail it up by the tail at a convenient height, or impale it thus on the sharpened end of a little stake; cut through the skin, around the body, just forward of the tail, work its edges loose, then pull, stripping off the skin entire. If preferred, the skin can be scalded.

Venison keeps a long time without curing, if the climate is cool and dry. To cure a deer's ham, hang it up by the shank, divide the muscles just above the hock, and insert a handful of dry salt. The meat of the deer tribe gets more tender and better flavored the longer it is hung up. In warm weather dust flour all over a haunch or saddle of venison, sew it up in a loose bag of cheesecloth, and hang it in a shady place where there is a current of air. It will keep sweet for several weeks, if there is no crevice in the bag through which insects can penetrate. Ordinarily it is best not to salt meat, for salt draws the juices. Bear meat, however, requires much salt to cure it— more than any other game animal. Hornaday recommends the following recipe for curing venison:—

The proportions of the mixture I use are:
        Salt ....3 lbs.,
        Allspice ....4 table-spoonfuls,
        Black Pepper ...5   "   "
        all thoroughly mixed.

Take a ham of deer, elk, or mountain sheep, or fall-killed mountain goat, and as soon as possible after killing, dissect the thigh, muscle by muscle. Any one can learn to do this by following up with the knife the natural divisions between the muscles. With big game like elk, some of the muscles of the thigh are so thick they require to be split in two. A piece of meat should not exceed five inches in thickness. Skin off all enveloping membranes, so that the curative powder will come in direct contact with the raw, moist flesh. The flesh must be sufficiently fresh and moist that the preservative will readily adhere to it. The best size for pieces of meat to be cured by this process is not over a foot long, by six or eight inches wide and four inches thick.

When each piece has been neatly and skilfully prepared rub the powder upon every part of the surface, and let the mixture adhere as much as it will. Then hang up each piece of meat, by a string through a hole in the smaller end, and let it dry in the wind. If the sun is hot, keep the meat in the shade; but in the North the sun helps the process. Never let the meat get wet. If the weather is rainy for a long period, hang your meat-rack where it will get heat from the campfire, but no more smoke than is unavoidable, and cover it at night with a piece of canvas.

Meat thus prepared is not at its best for eating until it is about a month old; then slice it thin. After that no sportsman, or hunter, or trapper can get enough of it. . . .

No; this is *not* "jerked" meat. It is many times better. It is always eaten uncooked, and as a concentrated, stimulating food for men in the wilds it is valuable.

(Hornaday. Camp-fires in the Canadian Rockies, 201-203.)

It is a curious fact that blow-flies work close to the ground, and will seldom meddle with meat that is hung more than ten feet above the ground. Game or fish suspended at a height of twenty feet will be immune from "blows."

To keep fish that must be carried some distance, in hot weather: clean them as soon as you can after they are caught, and *wipe them dry*. Then rub a little salt along their backbones, but nowhere else. Do not pile them touching each other, but between layers of cheesecloth, nettles, or basswood leaves.

To keep fish in camp: scale, clean, and behead them; then string them by a cord through their tails and hang them, head down, in a shady, dry, breezy place. Never use fish that have been lying in the sun or that have begun to soften. Ptomaine poisoning works in a mysterious but effectual way.

To dry fish for future use: split them along the back, remove the backbones and entrails, salt the fish, and hang them up on a frame over a smudge until they are well smoked. Or, make a trough by hewing out a softwood log, place the split fish in this, and cover them with a weak brine for one or two nights. Make a conical bark tepee on a tripod, suspend the fish in it, and dry and smoke them over a small fire for three days and nights.

To ship rabbits, squirrels, etc.: do not skin them, but remove the entrails, wipe the insides perfectly dry, wrap in paper, and pack them back down.

Never pack birds or fish in straw or grass without ice, for in damp or warm weather this will heat or sweat them. Do not let them freeze, as they will quickly spoil after thawing. Food in a bird's crop soon sours; the crop should be removed.

To preserve birds in warm weather for shipment: draw them, wash the inside perfectly clean, dry thoroughly, and then take pieces of charcoal from the fireplace, wrap them in a thin rag, and fill the abdominal cavity with this. Also fill the bill, ears, eyes, and anal opening with powdered charcoal, to keep off flies and prevent putrefaction. Reject all pieces of charcoal that are only half-burnt or have the odor of creosote. Birds stuffed in this way will keep sweet for a week in hot weather.

If you pack birds or fish in ice, wrap them first in many thicknesses of paper or grass, so that no ice can touch them.

CHAPTER V.

MEAT.

THE main secrets of good meals in camp are to have a proper fire, good materials, and then to imprison in each dish, at the outset, its natural juice and characteristic flavor. To season fresh camp dishes as a French chef would is a blunder of the first magnitude. The raw materials used in city cuisine are often of inferior quality, from keeping in cold storage or with chemical preservatives; so their insipidity must be corrected by spices, herbs, and sauces to make them eatable. In cheap restaurants and boarding houses, where the chef's skill is lacking, "all things taste alike" from having been penned up together in a refrigerator and cooked in a fetid atmosphere.

In my chapter on *Provisions* I advised that a few condiments be taken along, but these are mostly for seasoning left-overs or for desserts— not for fresh meat, unless we have but one kind, to the surfeiting point. In the woods our fish is freshly caught, our game has hung out of doors, and the water and air used in cooking (most important factors) are sweet and pure. Such viands need no masking. The only seasoning required is with pepper and salt, to be used sparingly, and not added (except in soups and stews) until the

49

dish is nearly or quite done. Remember this: salt draws the juices.

The juices of meats and fish are their most palatable and nutritious ingredients. We extract them purposely in making soups, stews, and gravies, but in so doing we ruin the meat itself. Any fish, flesh, or fowl that is fit to be eaten for the good meat's sake should be cooked succulent, by first coagulating the outside (searing in a bright flame or in a very hot pan, or plunging into smoking hot grease or furiously boiling water) and then removing farther from the fire to cook gradually till done. The first process, which is quickly performed, is "the surprise." It sets the juices, and, in the case of frying, seals the fish or meat in a grease-proof envelope so that it will not become sodden but will dry crisp when drained. The horrors of the frying-pan that has been unskillfully wielded are too well known. Let us campers, to whom the frying-pan is an almost indispensable utensil, set a good example to our grease-afflicted country by using it according to the code of health and epicurean taste.

Meat, game, and fish may be fried, broiled, roasted, baked, boiled, stewed, or steamed. Frying and broiling are the quickest processes; roasting, baking, and boiling take an hour or two; a stew of meat and vegetables, to be good, takes half a day, and so does soup prepared from the raw materials. Tough meat should be boiled or braised in a pot.

FRYING.

Do not try to fry over a flaming fire or a deep bed of coals; the grease would likely burn and catch aflame. Rake a thin layer of coals out in front of the fire; or, for a quick meal, make your fire of small dry sticks, no thicker than your finger, boil water for your coffee over the flame, and then fry over the quickly formed coals.

If you have a deep pan and plenty of frying fat, it is much the best to immerse the material completely in boiling grease, as doughnuts are fried. Let the fat boil until little jets of smoke arise (being careful not to burn the grease). When fat begins to smoke continuously it is decomposing and will impart an acrid taste. When a bread crumb dropped in will be crisp when taken out, the fat is of the right temperature. Then quickly drop in small pieces of the material, one at a time so as not to check the heat. Turn them once while cooking. Remove when done, and drop them a moment on coarse paper to absorb surplus grease, or hang them over a row of small sticks so they can drain. Then season. The fry will be crisp, and dry enough to handle without soiling the fingers. This is *the* way for small fish.

Travelers must generally get along with shallow pans and little grease. To fry (or, properly, to sauté) in this manner, without getting the article sodden and unfit for the stomach, heat the dry pan very hot, and then grease it only enough to keep the meat from sticking (fat meat needs none). The material must be dry when put in the pan (wipe fish with a towel) or it will absorb grease. Cook quickly and turn frequently, not jabbing with a fork for that would let juice escape. Season when done, and serve piping hot.

Fat used for frying fish must not be used again for anything but fish. Surplus fat can be kept in a baking powder can, sealed, for transit, with surgeon's plaster.

Chops, fat meats, squirrels, rabbits, and the smaller game birds are best sautéd or fricasseed and served with gravy. A fricassee is made of meat or birds cut into small pieces, fried or stewed, and served with gravy. Sausage should be fried over a very gentle fire.

BROILING.

Fresh meat that is tender enough to escape the boiling pot or the braising oven should either be broiled or roasted before a bed of clear, hard coals. Both of these processes preserve the characteristic flavor of the meat and add that piquant, aromatic-bitter "taste of the fire" which no pan nor oven can impart. Broil when you are in a hurry, but when you have leisure for a good job, roast your meat, basting it frequently with drippings from the pan below, so as to keep the surface moist and flexible and insure that precise degree of browning which delights a gourmet.

For broiling, cut the meat at least an inch thick. Only tender pieces are fit for broiling. Venison usually requires some pounding, but don't gash it in doing so. Have a bed of bright coals free from smoke, with clear flaming fire to one side. Sear outside of meat by thrusting for a moment in the flame and turning; then broil before the fire, rather than over it, so as to catch drippings in a pan underneath. Do not season until done. A steak 1 inch thick should be broiled five minutes, 1½ inches ten minutes, 2 inches twenty minutes. Serve on hot dish with drippings poured over, or buttered.

To broil enough for a party, when you have no

broiler, clean the frying-pan thoroughly and get it almost red hot, so as to seal pores of meat instantly. Cover pan. Turn meat often, without stabbing. A large venison steak will be done in ten minutes. Put on hot dish, season with pepper and salt, and pour juices over it. Equal to meat broiled on a gridiron, and saves the juices. To broil by completely covering the slice of meat with hot ashes and embers is a very good way.

To grill on a rock, take two large flat stones of a kind that do not burst from heat (not moist ones), wipe them clean of grit, place them one above the other, with a few pebbles between to keep them apart, and build a fire around them. When they are well heated, sweep away the ashes, and place your slices of meat between the stones.

Before broiling fish on an iron they should be buttered and floured to prevent sticking; or, grease the broiler.

ROASTING.

To roast is to cook by the direct heat of the fire, as on a spit or before a high bed of coals. Baking is performed in an oven, pit, or closed vessel. No kitchen range can compete with an open fire for roasting.

Build a rather large fire of split hardwood (softwoods are useless) against a high backlog or wall of rocks which will reflect the heat forward. Sear the outside of the roast (not a bird or fish) in clear flames until outer layer of albumen is coagulated. Then skewer thin slices of pork to upper end; hang roast before fire and close to it by a stout wet cord; turn frequently; catch drippings in pan or green-bark trough, and baste with them. This is better than roasting on a spit over the fire, because the heat can be better regulated, the meat turned and held in position more easily, the roast is not smoked, and the drippings are utilized.

Just before the meat is done, baste it and sprinkle with flour, then brown it near the fire, and make gravy as directed on page 62.

A whole side of venison can be roasted by planting two stout forked stakes before the fire, a stub of each stake being thrust through a slit cut between the ribs and under the backbone. The forward part of the saddle is the best roasting piece. Trim off flanky parts and ends of ribs, and split backbone lengthwise so that the whole will hang flat. To roast a shoulder, peel it from the side, cut off leg at knee, gash thickest part of flesh, press bits of pork into them, and skewer some slices to upper part.

When roasting a large joint, a turkey, or anything else that will require more than an hour of steady heat, do not depend upon adding wood from time to time, unless you have a good supply of sound, dry hardwood sticks of stove-wood size. If green wood or large sticks must be used, build a bonfire of them at one side of your cooking-fire, and shovel coals from it as required. It will not do to check the cooking-fire.

Kabobs.—When in a hurry, cut a 1½ or 2 inch portion from the saddle or other tender part, break up the fiber by pounding, unless the animal was young, and divide the meat into several small fragments. Impale one of these on a sharpened stick, salt and pepper it, plunge it for a moment into a clear bright flame, then toast it slowly over the embers. Salt, in this case, is glazed on the sur-

face and cannot draw the juice. While eating one
bit, toast another.

Roasting in the Reflector.—Pin thin slices of
pork or bacon over the roast. Put a little water
in the bake-pan, lay the meat in, and set the baker
before the fire. Baste occasionally. When the
front is done, reverse the pan. Make gravy from
the drippings.

Barbecueing.—To barbecue is to roast an animal whole, and baste it frequently with a special
dressing, for which the following recipe is bor-
rowed from Frank Bates:

One pint of vinegar, half a can of tomatoes, two teaspoonfuls of red pepper (chopped pepper-pods are better), a teaspoonful of black pepper, same of salt, two
tablespoonfuls of butter. Simmer together till it is completely amalgamated. Have a bit of clean cloth or
sponge tied on the end of a stick, and keep the meat
well basted with the dressing as long as it is on the fire.

BRAISING.

Tough meat is improved by braising in a Dutch
oven, or a covered pot or saucepan. This process
lies, between baking and frying. It is pre-emi-
nently the way to cook bear meat, venison shoul-
ders and rounds. Put the meat in the oven or
pot with about two inches of hot water in the bottom, and a bit of bacon or pork (but not for bear).
Add some chopped onion, if desired, for seasoning.
Cover and cook about fifteen minutes to the
pound. A half hour before the meat is done, season it with salt and pepper.

The gravy is made by pouring the grease from
the pot, adding a little water and salt, and rubbing
flour into it gradually with a spoon.

BAKING MEAT.

Baking in a Hole.—This is a modification of

braising. Dig a hole in the ground, say 18x18x12 inches. Place kindling in it, and over the hole build a cob house by laying split hardwood sticks across, not touching each other, then another course over these and at right angles to them, and so on till you have a stack two feet high. Set fire to it. The air will circulate freely, and the sticks, if of uniform size, will all burn down to coals together.

Cut the fowl, or whatever it is, in pieces, season, add a chunk of fat pork the size of your fist, put in the kettle, pour in enough water to cover, put lid on kettle, rake coals out of hole, put kettle in, shovel coals around and over it, cover all with a few inches of earth, and let it alone over night. It beats a bake-oven. In case of rain, cover with bark.

Experiment with this two or three times before you risk much on it; for the right heat and the time required can only be learned by experience.

Baking an Animal in its Hide.—If the beast is too large to bake entire, cut off what you want and sew it up in a piece of the hide. In this case it is best to have the hole lined with flat stones. Rake out embers, put meat in, cover first with, green grass or leaves, then with the hot coals and ashes, and build a fire on top. When done, remove the skin.

A deer's head is placed in the pit, neck down, and baked in the same way: time about six hours.

Baking in Clay.—This hermetically seals the meat while cooking, and is better than baking in a kettle, but requires experience. Draw the animal, but leave the skin and hair on. If it be a large bird, as a duck or goose, cut off head and most of neck, also feet and pinions, pull out tail

feathers and cut tail off (to get rid of oil sac),
but leave smaller feathers on. If a fish, do not
scale. Moisten and work some clay till it is like
softened putty. Roll it out in a sheet an inch or
two thick and large enough to completely encase
the animal. Cover the latter so that no feather
or hair projects. Place in fire and cover with good
bed of coals and let it remain with fire burning
on top for about ¾ of an hour, if a medium fish
or bird. Larger animals require more time, and
had best be placed in bake-hole over night.

When done, break open the hard casing of baked
clay. The skin peels off with it, leaving the meat
perfectly clean and baked to perfection in its own
juices. This method has been practiced for ages
by the gypsies and other primitive peoples.

Frank Bates recommends another way: "Have
a pail of water in which stir clay until it is of
the consistency of thick porridge or whitewash.
Take the bird by the feet and dip into the water.
The clay will gather on and between the feathers.
Repeat till the bird is a mass of clay. Lay this
in the ashes, being careful to dry the outside. . . .
Bake till the clay is almost burned to a brick."

Baking in the Embers.—To bake a fish, clean
it—if it is large enough to be emptied through a
hole in the neck, do not slit the belly—season
with salt and pepper, and, if liked, stuff with In-
dian meal. Have ready a good bed of glowing
hardwood coals; cover it with a thin layer of
ashes, that the fish may not be burnt. Lay the
fish on this, and cover it with more ashes and coals.
Half an hour, more or less, is required, according to size. On removing the fish, pull off the
skin, and the flesh will be found clean and palatable.

A bird, for example a duck, is baked in much the same way. Draw it, but do not remove the feathers. If you like stuffed duck, stuff with bread crumbs or broken biscuit, well seasoned with salt and pepper. Wet the feathers by dipping the bird in water; then bury it in the ashes and coals. A teal will require about half an hour; other birds in proportion.

BOILING.

The broader the pot, and the blacker it is, the quicker it boils. Fresh meats should be started in boiling water; salt or corned meats, and those intended for stews or soups, in cold water. The meat (except hams) should be cut into chunks of not over five pounds each, and soup bones well cracked. Watch during first half hour, and skim off all scum as fast as it rises, or it will settle and adhere to meat. Fresh meat should be boiled until bones are free, or until a fork will pierce easily (ten pounds take about two and a half hours). Save the broth for soup-stock, or make gravy of it by seasoning with pepper and thickening with flour. (See page 62.)

Meat that is to be eaten cold should be allowed to cool in the liquor in which it was boiled. A tablespoonful or two of vinegar added to the boiling water makes meat more tender and fish firmer. Turn the meat several times while boiling. If the water needs replenishing, do it with boiling, not cold, water. Season a short time before meat is done. If vegetables are to be cooked with the meat, add them at such time that they will just finish cooking when the meat is done (potatoes twenty to thirty minutes before the end; carrots and turnips, sliced, one to one and a half hours).

Remember this: put fresh meat in hard boiling water for only five minutes, to set the juices; then remove to greater height over the fire and boil very slowly—to let it boil hard all the time would make it tough and indigestible. Salt or corned meats go in cold water at the start and are gradually brought to a boil; thereafter they should be allowed barely to simmer.

Fish go in boiling salted water. Boiling meat must be kept covered.

At high altitudes it is impossible to cook satisfactorily by boiling, because water boils at a lower and lower temperature the higher we climb. The decrease is at the rate of about one degree for every 550 feet up to one mile, and one degree for 560 feet above that, when the temperature is 70°. With the air at 32° F., and the barometer at 30 inches, water boils at 212° at sea-level, 202.5° at 5,000 feet, 193.3° at 10,000 feet, and 184.5° at 15,000 feet. These figures vary somewhat according to the purity of the water, the material of the vessel, etc. To parboil is to boil only until tender, before cooking in some other way.

STEWING.

This process is slow, and should be reserved for tough meats. Use lean meat only. First brown it with some hot fat in a frying-pan; or put a couple of ounces of chopped pork in a kettle and get it thoroughly hot; cut your meat into small pieces; drop them into the fat and "jiggle" the kettle until the surface of the meat is coagulated by the hot fat, being careful, the while, not to burn it. Add a thickening of a couple of ounces of flour and mix it thoroughly with the fat; then a pint of water or soup-stock. Heat the contents

of the kettle to boiling and season with salt, pepper, and chopped onion. Curry powder, if you
like it, is proper in a stew. Now cover the kettle
closely and hang it where it will only simmer for
four or five hours. Stews may be thickened with
rice, potatoes, or oatmeal, as well as with flour.
Add condiments to suit the taste. A ragout is
nothing but a highly seasoned stew. The greater
the variety of meats and vegetables, the better.

The method given above is the one I have fol-
lowed; but I take the liberty of adding another
by Captain Kenealy:

Stewing is an admirable way of making palatable
coarse and tough pieces of meat, but it requires the
knack, like all other culinary processes. Have a hot fry-
pan ready, cut the meat up into small squares and put
it (without any dripping or fat) into the pan. Let it
brown well, adding a small quantity of granulated sugar
and sliced onions to taste. Cook until the onions are
tender and well colored. Then empty the fry-pan into a
stew-pan and add boiling water to cover the meat, and
let it simmer gently for two or three hours. Flavor with
salt, pepper, sweet herbs, curry powder or what you will.
The result will be a savory dish of tender meat, called by
the French a ragout. It is easy to prepare it this way.
Do not boil it furiously as is sometimes done, or it will
become tough. This dish may be thickened with browned
flour, and vegetables may be added—turnips, carrots,
celery, etc., cut into small pieces and browned with the
meat. The sugar improves the flavor vastly. The only
condiments actually necessary are pepper and salt.
Other flavorings are luxuries.

STEAMING.

To steam meat or vegetables: build a large fire
and throw on it a number of smooth stones, not
of the bomb-shell kind. Dig a hole in the ground
near the fire. When the stones are red hot, fork
them into the hole, level them, cover with green
or wet leaves, grass, or branches, place the meat
or potatoes on this layer, cover with more leaves.

and then cover all with a good layer of earth.
Now bore a small hole down to the food, pour
in some water, and immediately stop up the hole,
letting the food steam until tender. This is the
Chinook method of cooking camass. Shellfish can
be steamed in the same way.

MEAT GRAVIES AND SAUCES.

A gravy is seasoned with nothing but salt and
pepper, the object being to preserve the flavor
of the meat. A sauce is highly seasoned to disguise poor meat, or made-over dishes, or whatever
has been served so often that it begins to pall
on the appetite.

An abundance of rich gravy is relished by
campers who do not carry butter. They have
nothing else to make their bread "slip down."
Good gravy cannot be made from meat that has
been fried properly or broiled, because the juice
is left in the meat. Our pioneer families seldom
had butter, yet they had to eat a much larger
component of bread than we do, from lack of
side dishes. Hence the "fried-to-a-chip" school
of cookery.

In such case, the right way is obvious, granting
that you have plenty of meat. Fry properly
enough meat for the party and leave enough more
in the pan to make gravy. Gash or mince this
remainder, cook all the juice out of it without
scorching, throw out the refuse meat, rub in a
thickening prepared in advance as directed below,
salt and pepper, then thin to the desired consistency with boiling water. The thickening is
made by rubbing cold milk, or water, or broth, a
little at a time, into a spoonful of flour, until a
smooth paste is formed that will just drop from a

spoon; or thicken with roux. Chopped liver improves a gravy.

Roux (pronounced "roo") is a thickening for gravy or soups that can be prepared at any time and kept ready for emergencies. It will keep good for months in a covered jar. A teaspoonful thickens half a pint of gravy, or a pint of soup.

Brown roux is made thus: Melt slowly ½ lb. of butter, skim it well, let it stand for a minute to settle, and pour it off from the curd. Put the clear oily butter into a pan over a slow fire, shake into it enough sifted flour (7 or 8 oz.) to make a thick paste. Stir constantly and heat slowly and evenly until it is very thick and of a bright brown color. Put it into a jar. White roux is made in the same way except that it is stirred over a very gentle fire until it is thoroughly baked but not browned. It is used for white gravy on fish, etc.

Gravy for Boiled Meat.—Some of the liquor in which the meat was cooked can be thickened by melting a piece of butter the size of a small egg, mixing with it very smoothly a tablespoonful of flour, heating until lightly browned, adding the meat liquor and letting it boil up. Flavor to taste and serve separately from the meat.

Gravy for Roast Meat.—Use the drippings as above, and thin with boiling water in which half a teaspoonful of salt has been dissolved.

Dripping is the fat that drops from meat when roasting.

Gravy from Extract of Beef.—When there is no venison in camp, it will not be long before the men crave the taste of beef. Liebig's extract dissolved in boiling water and liberally salted will make a good beef gravy by letting it boil up, then simmer, and thicken in one of the ways described above.

Cream Gravy for Meat or Fish.—

½ pint milk.
1 tablespoonful butter.
½ tablespoonful flour.
½ tablespoonful salt.
⅛ tablespoonful pepper.

Heat butter in frying-pan. Add flour, stirring until smooth and frothy. Draw pan· back and gradually stir in the milk. Then return the pan to the fire. Add salt and pepper. Stir until sauce boils. This must be used at once, and everybody's plate should be hot, of course.

Sauces.—A camp cook nearly always lacks the sweet herbs, fresh parsley, mushrooms, capers, anchovies, shrimps, tarragon, wine, and many other condiments to which standard sauces owe their characteristic flavors. He must make shift with spices and perhaps lemon, Worcestershire, vinegar, mustard, curry powder, or celery seed. How to use these to the best advantage cannot be taught in a book. Personal tastes and the materials at hand must govern. I give here the recipes for three simple sauces for meat. Others will be found in the chapters on *Game, Fish,* and *Desserts.*

Mustard Sauce.—Brown two teaspoonfuls of flour in a pan with a little butter. Put two tablespoonfuls of butter on a plate and blend with it the browned flour, a teaspoonful of mustard, and a little salt. When these are smoothly mixed stir them into ¼ pint boiling water. Simmer five minutes. Add enough vinegar or lemon juice to flavor.

Venison Sauce.—Stir together one tablespoonful of butter with a teaspoonful of mustard and three

tablespoonfuls of jelly (preferably currant).
When these are well blended, add three tablespoonfuls of vinegar, some grated nutmeg, and
a dash of Cayenne pepper. Heat together.
When the sauce boils add three tablespoonfuls
chopped pickles. Serve at once. Currant jelly
alone goes well with venison.

Sauce for Broiled Venison.—Make the steak-dish
very hot. Put on it for each pound of venison ½
tablespoonful of butter, a tablespoonful of currant jelly, one of boiling water, and a little pepper and salt. Turn the broiled steaks in the
sauce once or twice and serve very hot.

CHAPTER VI.

GAME.

THE following additional details are supplementary to what has gone before, and presuppose a careful reading of the preceding pages.

Game and all other kinds of fresh meat should be hung up till they have bled thoroughly and have cooled through and through—they are tenderer and better after they have hung several days. Venison especially is tough until it has hung a week. In no case cook meat until the animal heat has left it: if you do, it is likely to sicken you. This does not apply to fish. Frozen meat or fish should be thawed in very cold water and then cooked immediately—warm water would soften it and steal its flavor.

All mammals from the coon size down, as well as duck and grouse, unless young and tender, or unless they have hung several days, should be parboiled (gently simmered) from ten to thirty minutes, according to size, before frying, broiling, or roasting. The scent glands of mammals and the oil sacs of birds should be removed before cooking. In small mammals look for pea-shaped, waxy or red kernels under the front legs and on either side of the small of the back.

As game has little natural fat, it requires frequent basting and the free use of butter or bacon grease in cooking.

65

(Deer of all species, elk, moose, caribou.)

Fried Venison.—See page 50.
Broiled Venison.—See page 52.
Roast Venison.—See page 53.
Braised Venison.—See page 55.
Baked Venison.—See page 55.
Boiled Venison.—See page 58.
Stewed Venison.—See page 59.
Steamed Venison.—See page 60.
Baked Deer's Head.—See page 56.

Deer's Brains.—Fry them; or boil slowly half an hour.

Heart.—Remove valves and tough, fibrous tissue; then braise, or cut into small pieces and use in soups or stews.

Kidneys.—Soak in cold water one hour. Cut into small pieces, and drop each piece into cold water, as cut. Wash well; then stew, seasoning with onion, celery seed, cloves, salt, pepper.

Liver.—Carefully remove gall-bladder, if the animal has one—deer have none. Parboil the liver and skim off the bitter scum that rises; then fry with bacon; or put the liver on a spit, skewer some of the caul fat around it, and roast before the fire; or cut the liver into slices ¼ inch thick, soak it one hour in cold salt water, rinse well in warm water, wipe dry, dip each slice in flour seasoned with salt and pepper, and fry.

Marrow Bones.—Cover ends with small pieces of plain dough made with flour and water, over which tie a floured cloth; place bones upright in kettle, and cover with boiling water. Boil two hours. Remove cloth and paste, push out marrow, and serve with dry toast.

Milt (Spleen).—Skewer a piece of bacon to it, and broil.

Moose Muffle.—Boil like pig's head. Add an onion.

Tongue.—Soak for one hour; rinse in fresh water; put in a kettle of cold water, bring to a boil, skim, and simmer two hours, or until tender. A blade of mace and a clove or two improve the gravy; so also Worcestershire sauce.

Venison Sausages.—Utilize the tougher parts of the deer, or other game, by mincing the raw meat with half as much salt pork, season with pepper and sage, make into little pats, and fry like sausages. Very good.

Game Pot Pie.—Take ½ teaspoonful baking powder to ½ pint of flour, sift together, and add a teaspoonful lard or butter by rubbing it in, also a pinch of salt. Make a soft biscuit dough of this, handling as little as possible and being careful not to mix too thin. Roll into a sheet and cut into strips about 1½ inch wide and 3 inches long, cutting two or three little holes through each to let steam escape. Meantime you have been boiling meat or game and have sliced some potatoes. When the meat is within one-half hour of being done, pour off the broth into another vessel and lift out most of the meat. Place a layer of meat and potatoes in bottom of kettle, and partially cover with strips of the dough; then another layer of meat and vegetables, another of dough, and so on until the pot is nearly full, topping off with dough. Pour the hot broth over this, cover tightly, and boil one-half hour, without lifting the pot cover, which, by admitting cold air, would make the dough "sad." Parsley helps the pot, when you can get it.

Dumplings.—These add zest to a stew or to boiled meat of any kind. Plain dumplings are

made of biscuit dough or the batter of dropped
biscuit (recipes in chapter on *Bread*). Drop them
into the pot a short time before meat is done.
See also page 117.

Bear, Braised.—See page 55.

Jambolaya.—This is a delicious Creole dish,
easily prepared. Cut up any kind of small game
into joints, and stew them. When half done, add
some minced ham or bacon, ¼ pint rice, and season with pepper and salt. If rabbit is used, add
onions. Serve with tomatoes as a sauce.

Brunswick Stew.—This famous huntsman's dish
of the Old Dominion is usually prepared with
squirrels, but other game will serve as well. The
ingredients, besides squirrels, are:

> 1 qt. can tomatoes,
> 1 pt. can butter beans or limas,
> 1 pt. can green corn,
> 6 potatoes, parboiled and sliced,
> ½ lb. butter,
> ½ lb. salt pork (fat),
> 1 teaspoonful black pepper,
> ½ teaspoonful Cayenne,
> 1 tablespoonful salt,
> 2 tablespoonfuls white sugar,
> 1 onion, minced small.

Soak the squirrels half an hour in cold salted
water. Add the salt to one gallon of water, and
boil five minutes. Then put in the onion, beans,
corn, pork (cut in fine strips), potatoes, pepper,
and squirrels. Cover closely, and stew very
slowly two and a half hours, stirring frequently
to prevent burning. Add the tomatoes and sugar
and stew an hour longer. Then add the butter,
cut into bits the size of a walnut and rolled in
flour. Boil ten minutes. Then serve at once.

Curry of Game.—Cut some birds or other small game into rather small joints. Fry until lightly browned. Score each joint slightly, place a little curry powder in each opening, and squeeze lemon juice over it. Cover the joints with brown gravy and simmer gently for twenty minutes. Serve with rice around the dish. (See also *Curry Sauce*, page 80.)

Game Pie.—Make a plain pie crust as directed in the chapter on *Desserts*. Cut the game into joints. Season rather highly. Moisten the joints with melted butter and lemon juice, or put a few thin strips of bacon in with them. Cover with top crust like a fruit pie and bake not too long; time according to size.

Squirrels, Fried.—Unless they are young, parboil them gently for ½ hour in salted water. Then fry in butter or pork grease until brown. A dash of curry powder when frying is begun improves them, unless you dislike curry. Make gravy as directed on page 63.

Squirrels, Broiled.—Use only young ones. Soak in cold salted water for an hour, wipe dry, and broil over the coals with a slice of bacon laid over each squirrel to baste it.

Squirrels, Stewed.—They are best this way, or fricasseed. For directions see pages 59 and 52.

Squirrels, Barbecued.—Build a hardwood fire between two large logs lying about two feet apart. At each end of the fire drive two forked stakes about fifteen inches apart, so that the four stakes will form a rectangle, like the legs of a table. The forks should all be about eighteen inches above the ground. Choose young, tender squirrels (if old ones must be used, parboil them until tender but not soft). Prepare spits by cutting stout switches of some wood that does not burn easily (sassafras is best—beware of poison sumach), peel them, sharpen the points, and harden them by thrusting for a few moments under the hot ashes. Impale each squirrel by thrusting a spit through flank, belly, and shoulder, on one' side, and another spit similarly on the other side, spreading out the sides, and, if necessary, cutting through the ribs, so that the squirrel will lie open and flat.

Lay two poles across the fire from crotch to crotch of the posts, and across these lay your spitted squirrels. As soon as these are heated through, begin basting with a piece of pork on the end of a switch. Turn the squirrels as required. Cook slowly, tempering the heat, if needful, by scattering ashes thinly over the coals; but remove the ashes for a final browning. When the squirrels are done, butter them and gash a little that the juices may flow.

Rabbit, or Hare.—Remove the head; skin and draw, cut out the waxy glands under the front legs where they join the body; soak in cold salted water for one hour; rinse in fresh cold water and wipe dry.

For frying, select only young rabbits, or parboil first with salt and pepper. Cut off legs at body joint, and cut the back into three pieces. Sprinkle with flour and fry brown on both sides. Remove rabbit to a dish kept hot over a few coals. Make a gravy as follows: Put into the pan a small onion previously parboiled and minced and add one cup boiling water. Stir in gradually one or two tablespoonfuls of browned flour; stir well, and let it boil one minute. Season with pepper, salt, and nutmeg. Pour it over the rabbit.

To roast in reflector: cut as above, lay a slice of pork on each piece, and baste frequently. The rabbit may be roasted whole before the fire.

To bake in an oven: stuff with a dressing made of bread crumbs, the heart and liver (previously parboiled in a small amount of water), some fat salt pork, and a small onion, all minced and mixed together, seasoned with pepper, salt, and nutmeg, and slightly moistened with the water in which heart and liver were parboiled. Sew up the opening closely; rub butter or dripping over rabbit, dredge with flour, lay thin slices of fat pork on back, and place it in pan or Dutch oven, back uppermost. Pour into pan a pint or more of boiling water (or stock, if you have it), and bake with very moderate heat, one hour, basting every few minutes if in pan, but not if in Dutch oven. Prepare a gravy with the pot juice, as directed above.

Rabbit is good stewed with onion, nutmeg, pepper, and salt for seasoning. Also curried, after the manner already described.

Rabbits are unfit to eat in late summer, as their backs are then infested with warbles, which are the larvæ of the rabbit bot-fly.

Possum.—To call our possum an opossum, outside of a scientific treatise, is an affectation. Possum is his name wherever he is known and hunted, this country over. He is not good until you have freezing weather; nor is he to be served without sweet potatoes, except in desperate extremity. This is how to serve "possum hot."—

Stick him, and hang him up to bleed until morning. A tub is half filled with hot water (not quite scalding) into which drop the possum and hold him by the tail until the hair will strip. Take

him out, lay him on a plank, and pull the hair
out with your fingers. Draw, clean, and hang him
up to freeze for two or three nights. Then place
him in a 5-gallon kettle of cold water, into which
throw two pods of red pepper. Parboil for one
hour in this pepper-water, which is then thrown
out and the kettle refilled with fresh water,
wherein he is boiled one hour.

While this is going on, slice and steam some
sweet potatoes. Take the possum out, place him
in a large Dutch oven, sprinkle him with black
pepper, salt, and a pinch or two of sage. A
dash of lemon will do no harm. Pack sweet potatoes around him. Pour a pint of water into the
oven, put the lid on, and see that it fits tightly.
Bake slowly until brown and crisp. Serve hot,
without gravy. Bourbon whiskey is the only
orthodox accompaniment. If you are a teetotaler,
any plantation darky can show you how to make
"ginger tea" out of ginger, molasses, and water.
Corn bread, of course.

It is said that possum is not hard to digest even
when eaten cold, but the general verdict seems to
be that none is ever left over to get cold.

When you have no oven, roast the possum before a high bed of coals, having suspended him by
a wet string, which is twisted and untwisted to
give a rotary motion, and constantly baste it with
a sauce made from red pepper, salt, and vinegar.

Possum may also be baked in clay, with his
hide on. Stuff with stale bread and sage, plaster
over him an inch of stiff clay, and bake as previously directed. He will be done in about an hour.

Coon.—It is likewise pedantic to call this animal a raccoon. Coon he always has been, is now,
and shall ever be, to those who know him best.

Skin and dress him. Remove the "kernels" (scent glands) under each front leg and on either side of spine in small of back. Wash in cold water. Parboil in one or two waters, depending upon the animal's age. Stuff with dressing like a turkey. If you have a tart apple, quarter it and add to the dressing. Roast to a delicate brown. Serve with fried sweet potatoes.

Porcupine.—I quote from Nessmuk: "And do not despise the fretful porcupine; he is better than he looks. If you happen on a healthy young specimen when you are needing meat, give him a show before condemning him. Shoot him humanely in the head, and dress him. It is easily done; there are no quills on the belly, and the skin peels as freely as a rabbit's. Take him to camp, parboil him for thirty minutes, and roast or broil him to a rich brown over a bed of glowing coals. He will need no pork to make him juicy, and you will find him very like spring lamb, only better."

The porcupine may also be baked in clay, without skinning him; the quills and skin peel off with the hard clay covering. Or, fry *quickly.*

As I have never eaten porcupine, I will do some more quoting—this time from Dr. Breck: "It may be either roasted or made into a stew, in the manner of hares, but must be parboiled at least a half-hour to be tender. One part of the porcupine is always a delicacy—the *liver,* which is easily removed by making a cut just under the neck into which the hand is thrust, and the liver pulled out. It may be fried with bacon, or baked slowly and carefully in the baker-pan with slices of bacon."

Muskrat.—You may be driven to this, some day, and will then learn that muskrat, properly prepared, is not half bad. The French-Canadians found that out long ago.

"Skin and clean carefully four muskrats, being particular not to rupture musk or gall sac. Take the hind legs and saddles, place in pot with a little water, a little julienne (or fresh vegetables, if you have them), some pepper and salt, and a few slices of pork or bacon. Simmer slowly over fire until half done. Remove to baker, place water from pot in the baking pan, and cook until done, basting frequently. This will be found a most toothsome dish."

Muskrat may also be broiled over the hot coals, basting with a bit of pork held on a switch above the beastie.

Woodchuck.—I asked old Uncle Bob Flowers, one of my neighbors in the Smokies: "Did you ever eat a woodchuck?"

"Reckon I don't know what them is."

"Ground-hog."

"O la! dozens of 'em. The red ones hain't good, but the gray ones! man, they'd jest make yer mouth water!"

"How do you cook them?"

"Cut the leetle red kernels out from under their forelegs; then bile 'em, fust—all the strong is left in the water—then pepper 'em, and sage 'em, and put 'em in a pan, and bake 'em to a nice rich brown, and—then I don't want nobody there but me!"

Beaver Tail.—This tid-bit of the old-time trappers will be tasted by few of our generation, more's the pity! Impale the tail on a sharp stick and broil over the coals for a few minutes. The rough, scaly hide will blister and come off in sheets, leaving the tail clean, white, and solid.

Then roast, or boil until tender. It is of a gelatinous nature, tastes somewhat like pork, and is considered very strengthening food. A young beaver, stuffed and baked in its hide, is good; old ones have a peculiar flavor that is unpleasant to those not accustomed to such diet.

Beaver tail may also be soused in vinegar, after boiling, or baked with beans. The liver, broiled on a stick and seasoned with butter, salt, and pepper, is the best part of the animal.

BIRDS.

Game Birds, Fried.—Birds for frying should be cut in convenient pieces, parboiled until tender in a pot with enough water to cover, then removed, saving the liquor. Sprinkle with salt, pepper, and flour (this for the sake of the gravy), fry in melted pork fat, take out when done, then stir into the frying fat one-half cupful dry flour till a dark brown, add parboiling liquor, bring to a boil, put game in dish, and pour gravy over it, or serve with one of the sauces described below.

Game Birds, Broiled.—Split them up the back, broil over the coals, and baste with a piece of pork on tined stick held over them. Fillets of ducks or other large birds may be sliced off and impaled on sticks with thin slices of pork.

Game Birds, Fricasseed.—Any kind of bird may be fricasseed as follows: Cut it into convenient pieces, parboil them in enough water to cover; when tender, remove from the pot and drain. Fry two or three slices of pork until brown. Sprinkle the pieces of bird with salt, pepper, and flour, and fry to a dark brown in the pork fat. Take up the bird, and stir into the frying fat half a cup, more or less, of dry flour, stirring until it becomes a dark brown; then pour over it the liquor in which the bird was boiled (unless it was a fish-eater), and bring the mixture to a boil. Put the bird in a hot dish, and pour gravy over it.

Wild Turkey, Roasted.—Pluck, draw, and singe. Wipe the bird inside and out. Rub the inside with salt and red pepper. Stuff the crop cavity, then the body, with either of the dressings mentioned below, allowing room for the filling to swell. Tie a string around the neck, and sew up the body. Truss wings to body with wooden skewers. Pin thin slices of fat pork to breast in same way. Suspend the fowl before a high bed of hardwood coals, as previously described, and place a pan under it to catch drippings. Tie a clean rag on the end of a stick to baste with. Turn and baste frequently. Roast until well done (two to three hours). (See also page 53.)

Meantime cleanse the gizzard, liver, and heart of the turkey thoroughly in cold water; mince them; put them in a pot with enough cold water to cover, and stew gently until tender; then place where they will keep warm until wanted. When the turkey is done, add the giblets with the water in which they were stewed to the drippings in pan; thicken with one or two tablespoonfuls of flour that has been stirred up in milk or water and browned in a pan; season with pepper and salt, and serve with the turkey. If you have butter, the fowl may be basted with it (melted, of course), and when stewing the giblets add a tablespoonful of butter and half a teacupful of evaporated milk.

Stuffing for Turkey.—(1) If chestnuts are procurable, roast a quart of them, remove shells, and mash. Add a teaspoonful of salt, and some pep-

per. Mix well together, and stuff the bird with
them.

(2) Chop some fat salt pork very fine; soak
stale bread or crackers in hot water, mash smooth,
and mix with the chopped pork. Season with
salt, pepper, sage, and chopped onion. No game
bird save the wild turkey should be stuffed, unless
you deliberately wish to disguise the natural flavor.

Wild Turkey, Boiled.—Pluck, draw, singe, wash
inside with warm water, and wipe dry. Cut on
head and neck close to backbone, leaving enough
skin to turn over the stuffing. Draw sinews from
legs, and cut off feet just below joint of leg.
Press legs into sides and skewer them firmly.
Stuff breast as above. Put the bird into enough
hot water to cover it. Remove scum as it rises.
Boil gently one and one-half to two hours. Serve
with giblet sauce as above.

Waterfowl have two large oil glands in the tail,
with which they oil their feathers. The oil in
these glands imparts a strong, disagreeable flavor
to the bird soon after it is killed. Hence the tail
should always be removed before cooking.

To cook a large bird in a hurry.—Slice off several fillets from the breast; impale them, with
slices of pork, on a green switch; broil over the
coals.

Wild Goose, Roasted.—A good way to suspend
a large bird before the fire is described by Dillon
Wallace in his *Lure of the Labrador Wild:*

George built a big fire—much bigger than usual. At
the back he placed the largest green log he could find.
Just in front of the fire, and at each side, he fixed
a forked stake, and on these rested a cross-pole. From
the center of the pole he suspended a piece of stout
twine, which reached nearly to the ground, and tied the
lower end into a noose.

Then it was that the goose, nicely prepared for the

cooking, was brought forth. Through it at the wings George stuck a sharp wooden pin, leaving the ends to protrude on each side. Through the legs 'he stuck a similar pin in a similar fashion. This being done, he slipped the noose at the end of the twine over the ends of one of the pins. And lo and behold! the goose was suspended before the fire.

It hung low—just high enough to permit the placing of a dish under it to catch the gravy. Now and then George gave it a twirl so that none of its sides might have reason to complain at not receiving its share of the heat. The lower end roasted first; seeing which, George took the goose off, reversed it, and set it twirling again.

Time-table for Roasting Birds.—A goose or a middling-sized turkey takes about two hours to roast, a large turkey three hours, a duck about forty-five minutes, a pheasant twenty to thirty minutes, a woodcock or snipe fifteen to twenty minutes.

Wild Duck, Baked.—The bird should be dry-picked, and the head left on. Put a little pepper and salt inside the bird, but *no other dressing.* Lay the duck on its back in the bake-pan. Put no water in the pan. The oven must be hot, but not hot enough to burn; test with the hand. Baste frequently with butter or bacon. A canvasback requires about thirty minutes; other birds according to size. When done, the duck should be plump, and the flesh red, not blue.

This is the way to bring out the distinctive flavor of a canvasback. Seasoning and stuffing destroy all that. A canvasback should not be washed either inside or outside, but wiped clean with a dry cloth. Duck should be served with currant jelly, if you have it. (See also page 55.)

Wild Duck, Stewed.—Clean well and divide into convenient pieces (say, legs, wings, and four parts of body). Place in pot with enough cold water to cover. Add salt, pepper, a pinch of mixed herbs, and a dash of Worcestershire sauce. Cut up fine some onions and potatoes (carrots, too, if you can get them). Put a few of these in the pot so they may dissolve and add body to the dish (flour or corn starch may be substituted for thickening). Stew slowly, skim and stir frequently. In forty-five minutes add the rest of the carrots, and in fifteen minutes more add the rest of the onions and potatoes, also turnips, if you have any. Stew until meat is done.

A plainer camp dish is to stew for an hour in water that has previously been boiled for an hour with pieces of salt pork. (See also page 59.)

Fish-eating Ducks.—The rank taste of these can be neutralized, unless very strong, by baking with an onion inside. Use plenty of pepper, inside and out.

Mud-hens and Bitterns.—Remove the breast of a coot or rail, cut slits in it, and in these stick thin slices of fat salt pork; broil over the embers. The broiled breast of a young bittern is good.

Grouse, Broiled.—Pluck and singe. Split down the back through the bone, and remove the trail. Wipe out with damp towel. Remove head and feet. Rub inside with pepper and salt. Flatten the breast, brush over with melted butter, or skewer bacon on upper side, and grill over a hot bed of coals.

Grouse, Roasted.—Dress and draw, but do not split. Place a piece of bacon or pork inside, and skewer a piece to the breast. Roast before the fire as described for turkey, or in a reflector.

Small Birds (quail, woodcock, snipe, plover, etc.).—These are good roasted before a big bed of coals, searing them first as in broiling meat.

Impale each bird on a green stick, with a slice of
bacon on the point of the stick over the bird.
Thrust butt of stick into the ground, and incline
stick toward the fire. Turn frequently.

When a number of birds are to be roasted, a
better way is to set up two forked stakes and a
cross-pole before the fire. Hang birds from the
pole, heads downward, by wet strings. Baste as
recommended for turkey, and turn frequently.
Serve very hot, without any sauce, unless it be
plain melted butter and a slice of lemon.

Such birds can also be served in a ragout. (See
page 60.)

Woodcock are not drawn. The trail shrivels up
and is easily removed at table.

SAUCES FOR GAME. (See also page 63.)

Giblet Sauce.—See under *Wild Turkey,
Roasted.*

Celery Sauce.—Having none of the vegetable
itself, use a teaspoonful of celery seed freshly
powdered, or five drops of the essence of celery on
a piece of sugar. Flavor some melted butter
with this, add a little milk, and simmer ten minutes.

Cranberry Sauce.—Put a pound of ripe cranberries in a kettle with just enough water to prevent burning. Stew to a pulp, stirring all the
time. Then add syrup previously prepared by
boiling a pound of sugar in 2/3 pint of water.
Canned cranberries will answer.

Curry Sauce.—This is used with stewed small
game or meat (especially left-overs) that is served
in combination with rice. (See page 69.)

Put a large spoonful of butter in a pan over
the fire; add one onion cut into slices; cook until
the onion is lightly browned. Then stir in one

teaspoonful of curry powder and add gradually a
generous cup of brown gravy, or soup stock, or
the broth in which meat has been stewed, or
evaporated milk slightly thinned. Boil fifteen
minutes, and strain. Curry may be varied indefinitely by further flavoring with lemon juice,
red pepper, nutmeg, mace, or Worcestershire
sauce.

CHAPTER VII.

FISH AND SHELLFISH.

FISH of the same species vary a great deal in quality according to the water in which they are caught. A black bass taken from one of the overflow lakes of the Mississippi bears no comparison with its brother from a swift, clear, spring-fed Ozark river.

When it is necessary to eat fish caught in muddy streams, rub a little salt down the backbone, lay them in strong brine for a couple of hours before cooking, and serve with one of the sauces described farther on in this chapter. Carp should have the gills removed, as they are always muddy from burrowing.

Never put fish on a stringer to keep in water till you start for home. It is slow death for them, like putting a cord through an animal's lung and letting him half smother, half bleed to death. If you have no live-box or net, kill and bleed every fish as soon as caught. The flesh will be much firmer and more palatable.

Fish, Fried.—(See also page 50.) Small fish should be fried whole, with the backbone severed to prevent curling up; large fish should be cut into pieces, and ribs cut loose from backbone, so as to lie flat in pan. Rub the pieces in corn meal, or powdered crumbs, thinly and evenly (that browns them). Fry in plenty of very hot grease

82

to a golden brown, sprinkling lightly with pepper and salt just as the color turns. If the fish is not naturally full-flavored, a few drops of lemon juice will improve it.

Olive oil is best to fry fish in; the next choice is clear drippings or butter. If the fish has not been wiped dry it will absorb too much grease. If the frying fat is not very hot when fish are put in they will be soggy with it.

Fish, Broiled.—(See also page 52.) If a broiling iron is used, first rub it with fat bacon to prevent fish from sticking to it. In broiling large fish, remove the head, split down the back instead of the belly, and lay on the broiler with strips of bacon or pork laid across. Broil over a rather moderate bed of coals so that the inside will cook done. Small fish are best broiled quickly over ardent coals. They need not have heads removed.

When done, sprinkle with salt and pepper, spread with butter (unless you have used bacon), and hold again over fire until butter melts.

Fish, Skewered.—Small fish may be skewered on a thin, straight, greenwood stick, sharpened at the end, with a thin slice of bacon or pork between every two fish, the stick being constantly turned over the coals like a spit, so that juices may not be lost.

Another way is to cut some green hardwood sticks, about three feet long, forked at one end, and sharpen the tines. Lay a thin slice of pork inside each fish lengthwise, drive tines through fish and pork, letting them through between ribs near backbone and on opposite sides of the latter—then the fish won't drop off as soon as it begins to soften and curl from the heat. Place a log lengthwise of edge of coals, lay broiling sticks on this support, slanting upward over the fire, and lay a small log over their butts. Large fish should be planked.   ·

Fish Roasted in a Reflector.—This process is simpler than baking, and superior in resulting flavor, since the fish is basted in its own juices, and is delicately browned by the direct action of the fire. The surface of the fish is lightly moistened with olive·oil (first choice) or butter; lacking these, use drippings, or bacon grease, or lard. Then place the fish in the pan and add two or three morsels of grease around it. Roast in front of a good fire, just as you would bake biscuit. Be careful not to overroast and dry the fish by evaporating the gravy. There is no better way to cook a large fish, unless it be planked.

Fish, Planked.—More expeditious than baking, and better flavored. Split and smooth a slab of sweet hardwood two or three inches thick, two feet long, and somewhat wider than the opened fish. Prop it in front of a bed of coals till it is sizzling hot. Split the fish down the back its entire length, but do not cut through the belly skin. Clean and wipe it quite dry. When plank is hot, spread fish out like an opened book, tack it, skin side down, to the plank and prop before fire. Baste continuously with a bit of pork on a switch held above it. Reverse ends of plank from time to time. If the flesh is flaky when pierced with a fork, it is done. Sprinkle salt and pepper over the fish, moisten with drippings, and serve on the hot plank. No better dish ever was set before an epicure. Plenty of butter improves it at table.

Fish, Stuffed and Baked.—Clean, remove fins, but leave on head and tail. Prepare a stuffing as follows: put a cupful of dry bread-crumbs in a frying-pan over the fire with two tablespoonfuls of drippings, or the equivalent of butter, and stir them until they begin to brown. Then add enough boiling water to moisten them. Season this stuffing rather highly with salt, pepper, and either celery seed, or sage, or a teaspoonful of highly chopped onion. Stuff the fish with this and sew up the opening, or wind string several times around the fish. Lay several strips of salt pork or bacon in the pan, and several over the top of the fish. Sprinkle over all a little water, pepper, salt, and bread crumbs (or dredge with flour). Bake in a hot oven, basting frequently. When flakes of fish begin to separate, it will be done. This is best for coarse fish.

Fish Baked in Clay.—"Take a fresh-caught fish and rub it in soft clay from the river bank, against the scales and gills. When the clay is set a little, roll the whole fish in a blanket of clay, till the body is completely covered. Dry in the heat of the fire for fifteen minutes; bury in the hot coals and ashes till the clay is hard. Rake the brick out of the fire and crack it open with the hatchet. The fish will split in two pieces; the spine can easily be taken out; the 'inwards' are shrunk to a little ball, which can be flipped off; and the scales are stuck on the clay. Dust on a little salt, and you have a meal fit for—a hungry hunter." (*Frank Bates.*)

Fish, Steamed.—Smear some tissue Manila paper with butter. Clean the fish, leaving head and fins on. Season with salt and Cayenne pepper. Roll each fish separately in a piece of the buttered paper. Place the fish in a pile and envelop them in a large sheet of paper. Then wrap the bundle in a newspaper, and dip this in water for five minutes, or long enough to saturate the newspaper. Scrape a hole in the middle of a bed of coals, and bury the package in the embers. Leave it there ten to twenty minutes, depending upon size. The newspaper will scorch, but the inner wrappers will not. The result is a dish fit for Olympus. (*Up De Graff.*)

Small fish can be steamed in wet basswood leaves, or other large leaves, without buttering. For another method of steaming, see page 60.

Fish, Boiled.—None but fish of good size should be boiled. If the fish is started in cold water and not allowed to boil hard, it will be less likely to fall apart, but the flavor will not be so good. It is better to wrap the fish in a clean cloth and drop it into boiling water well salted. A tablespoonful of vinegar, or the juice of a lemon, improves the dish. Leave the head on, but remove the fins. Boil very gently until the flesh will easily part from the bones. Time depends on species; from eight to ten minutes per pound for thick fish, and five minutes for small ones.

Boiled fish require considerable seasoning and a rich sauce, or at least melted butter, to accompany them. Besides vinegar or lemon, onions, carrots, cloves, etc., may be used in the water. Recipes for sauces follow. (See also pages 63 and 80.)

Butter Sauce.—

    2 heaped tablespoonfuls butter.
    1 heaped tablespoonful flour.
    1 teaspoonful salt.
    ⅛ teaspoonful pepper.

Put the butter in a cold pan, and rub into it the flour, salt, and pepper, beating well. Then pour on a scant half-pint boiling water. Cook two minutes. Use immediately.

White Sauce.—

> 2 tablespoonfuls butter.
> 2 heaped tablespoonfuls flour.
> 1 pint milk.
> ½ teaspoonful salt.
> ⅛ teaspoonful pepper.

Cook butter until it bubbles. Add flour, and cook thoroughly. Remove from direct heat of fire, but let it simmer, and add the milk in thirds, rubbing into a smooth paste each time as it thickens. Season last.

Cold fish that has been left over is good when heated in this sauce. It can be served thus, or baked and some chopped pickles sprinkled over the top.

India Sauce.—Make a white sauce as above, add a teaspoonful of curry powder, and some pickles, chopped small, with a little of the vinegar.

Lemon Sauce.—

> 1 lemon.
> 3 tablespoonfuls sugar.
> ½ pint milk.
> 1 scant tablespoonful butter.

Put the milk, sugar, and thin rind of the lemon into a pan and simmer gently ten minutes. Then add the juice of the lemon and the butter rolled in flour. Stir until butter is dissolved and strain or pour off clear.

Fish Chowder.—Cut the fish into pieces the right size for serving, and remove all the bones possible. For 5 or 6 lbs. of fish take ¾ lb. clear fat salt pork, slice it, and fry moderately. Slice two good-sized onions and fry in the fat. Have ready ten potatoes pared and sliced. Into your largest pot place first a layer of fish, then one of potatoes, then some of the fried onion, with pepper, salt, and a little flour, then a slice or two of the pork. Repeat these alternate layers until

all has been used. Then pour the fat from the
frying-pan over all. Cover the whole with boiling
water, and cook from twenty to thirty minutes,
according to thickness of fish. Five or ten minutes
before serving, split some hard crackers and dip
them in cold water (or use stale bread or biscuits
similarly), add them to the chowder, and pour
in about a pint of hot milk.

The advantage of first frying the pork and
onion is that the fish need not then be cooked over-
done, which is the case in chowders started with
raw pork in the bottom of the kettle and boiled.

Another Fish Chowder.—Clean the fish, parboil
it, and reserve the water in which it was boiled.
Place the dry pot on the fire; when it is hot, throw
in a lump of butter and about six onions sliced
finely. When the odor of onion arises, add the
fish. Cover the pot closely for fish to absorb
flavor. Add a very small quantity of potatoes, and
some of the reserved broth. When cooked, let
each man season his own dish. Ask a blessing and
eat. (*Kenealy.*)

Fish Cakes.—Take fish left over from a previous
meal and either make some mashed potatoes (boil
them, and mash with butter and milk) or use just
the plain cold boiled potatoes. Remove bones from
fish and mince it quite fine. Mix well, in proportion of one-third fish and two-thirds potato. Season with salt and pepper. Then mix in thoroughly a well-beaten egg or two (or equivalent of
desiccated egg). If it seems too dry, add more
egg. Form into flat cakes about 2½ x ¾ inches,
and fry with salt pork, or (preferably) in deep
fat, like doughnuts.

Fish, Creamed.—See page 98. A good way of
utilizing fish left over.

Eel, Broiled.—Skin, clean well with salt to re-move slime, slit down the back and remove bone, cut into good-sized pieces, rub inside with egg, if you have it, roll in corn meal or dry bread-crumbs, season with pepper and salt, and broil to a nice brown. Some like a dash of nutmeg with the seasoning.

Eel, Stewed.—Skin the eel, remove backbone, and cut the eel into pieces about two inches long; cover these with water in the stew-pan, and add a teaspoonful of strong vinegar or a slice of lemon, cover stew-pan and boil moderately one half hour. Then remove, pour off water, drain, add fresh water and vinegar as before, and stew until tender. Now drain, add cream enough for a stew, season with pepper and salt (no butter), boil again for a few minutes, and serve on hot, dry toast. (*Up De Graff.*)

Fish Roe.—Parboil (merely simmer) fifteen minutes; let them cool and drain; then roll in flour, and fry.

MISCELLANEOUS.

Frog Legs.—First after skinning, soak them an hour in cold water to which vinegar has been added, or put them for two minutes into scalding water that has vinegar in it. Drain, wipe dry, and cook as below:

To fry: roll in flour seasoned with salt and pep-per and fry, not too rapidly, preferably in butter or oil. Water cress is a good relish with them.

To grill: Prepare three tablespoonfuls melted butter, one-half teaspoonful salt, and a pinch or two of pepper, into which dip the frog legs, then roll in fresh bread crumbs, and broil for three minutes on each side,

Turtles.—All turtles (aquatic) and most tortoises (land) are good to eat, the common snapper being far better than he looks. Kill by cutting throat or (readier) by shooting the head off. This does not kill the brute immediately, of course, but it suffices. The common way of killing by dropping a turtle into boiling water I do not like. Let the animal bleed. Then drop into a pot of boiling water for a few seconds. After scalding, the outer scales of shell, as well as the skin, are easily re-moved. Turn turtle on its back, cut down middle of under shell from end to end, and then across. Throw away entrails, head, and claws. Salt and pepper it inside and out. Boil a short time in the shell. Remove when the meat has cooked free from the shell. Cut up the latter and boil slowly for three hours with some chopped onion. If a stew is preferred, add some salt pork cut into dice, and vegetables. (See page 59.)

Crayfish.—These are the "craw-feesh!" of our streets. Tear off extreme end of tail, bringing the entrail with it. Boil whole in salted water till the crayfish turns red. Peel and eat as a lobster, dipping each crayfish at a time into a saucer of vinegar, pepper, and salt.

SHELLFISH.

Oysters, Stewed.—Oysters should not be pierced with a fork, but removed from the liquor with a spoon. Thoroughly drain the juice from a quart of shelled oysters. Add to the juice enough water (if needed) to make one-half pint. Place juice over fire, and add butter the size of a walnut. Remove all scum that arises when the juice boils. Put in the oysters. Let them cook quickly until the beards wrinkle, but not until oysters shrivel—they should remain plump. Add two-thirds pint of milk, let all scald through, remove from fire, and season to taste. Never boil oysters in milk.

Oysters, Fried.—Drain the oysters, and dry them on a soft cloth (then they will not absorb grease). Have some desiccated egg prepared, or beat light the yolks of two or three eggs. Have enough smoking hot grease in the pan to cover all the oysters. Dip an oyster into the egg, then into rolled cracker or dry crumbs, and repeat this. Lay oysters in the pan one at a time, so as not to check the heat. When one side is brown, turn, and brown the other side. Serve piping hot.

Oysters, Scalloped.—Cover bottom of greased bake-pan with a layer of drained oysters, dot thickly over with small bits of butter, then cover with finely crumbled stale bread, and sprinkle with pepper and salt. Repeat these layers until the pan is full, with bread and butter for top layer. The bread crumbs must be in very thin layers. Bake in reflector or oven until nicely browned.

Oysters, Sauté.—Drain the oysters. Melt a little butter in the frying-pan, and cook the oysters in it. Salt when removed from pan.

Oysters, Roasted.—Put oysters unopened on broiler, and hold over the coals. When they open, put a little melted butter and some white pepper on each oyster, and they are ready.

Clams, Baked.—Lay down a bed of stones in disk shape, and build a low wall almost around it, forming a rock oven open at the top. Build a big fire in it and keep it going until the wood has burned down to embers and the stones are very hot. Rake out all smoking chunks. Throw a layer of sea-weed over the embers, and lay the clams

on this. Roasting ears in the husks, or sweet potatoes, are a desirable addition. Cover all with
another layer of sea-weed, and let steam about
forty minutes, or until clams will slip in the shell.
Uncover and serve with melted butter, pepper,
salt, and perhaps lemon or vinegar.

Clam Chowder.—Wash the clams, put them in a
kettle, and pour over them just enough boiling
water to cover them. When the shells open, pour
off the liquor, saving it, cool the clams, and shell
them. Fry two or three slices of pork in bottom of kettle. When it is done, pour over it two
quarts of boiling clam liquor. Add six large potatoes, sliced thin, and cook until nearly done. Turn
in the clams, and a quart of hot milk. Season with
salt and pepper. When this boils up, add crackers
or stale bread, as in fish chowder. Remove from
fire and let crackers steam in the covered pot until soft.

Fried sliced onion and a can of tomatoes will
improve this chowder. Cloves, allspice, red pepper, Worcestershire sauce, and other condiments,
may be added according to taste.

Shellfish, Steamed.—See page 60.

CHAPTER VIII.

CURED MEATS, ETC.—EGGS.

BACON, *Fried.*—Slice quite thin. Remove the rind, as it not only is unsightly but makes the slices curl up in the pan. Put pan half full of water on fire; when water is warm, drop the bacon in, and stir around until water begins to simmer. Then remove bacon, throw out water, fry over very few coals, and turn often. Remove slices while still translucent, and season with pepper. They will turn crisp on cooling. Some prefer not to parboil.

Bacon, Broiled.—Slice as above. Turn broiler repeatedly until bacon is of a light brown color. Time, three to four minutes.

Bacon, Boiled.—Put in enough cold water to just cover. Bring to a boil very gradually. Remove all scum as it arises. Simmer gently until thoroughly done. Two pounds take 1½ hours; each additional pound, ½ hour.

Bacon, Toasted.—Cut cold boiled bacon into thin slices. Sprinkle each with fine bread crumbs peppered with Cayenne. Toast quickly in wire broiler.

Bacon and Eggs.—Poach or fry the eggs and lay them on fried bacon.

Bacon Omelet.—See *Ham Omelet,* near end of chapter.

Bacon and Liver.—Fry bacon as above, and re-

93

move to a hot plate. Slice the liver (that of any large game animal) thin. Flour and pepper it and place it in the pan. Turn frequently until done; then place a slice of bacon on each slice of liver and pour over it a gravy made as follows:

Bacon Gravy, Thin.—Pour off the fat and save it for future use. Pour in enough water to supply the quantity of gravy desired. Add the juice of a lemon. Boil and pour upon the bacon. If a richer gravy is desired, follow recipe given below.

Pork Gravy, Thickened.—This can be made with ham or salt pork, as well as with bacon. To make gravy that is a good substitute for butter, rub into the hot grease that is left in the pan a tablespoonful of flour, keep on rubbing until smooth and brown; then add two cups boiling water and a dash of pepper. A tablespoonful of catchup may be added for variety. If you have milk, use it instead of water (a pint to the heaping tablespoonful of flour), and do not let the flour brown; this makes a delicious white gravy.

Salt Pork, Fried.—Same as fried bacon, above. Pork should be firm and dry. Clammy pork is stale.

Salt Pork, Broiled.—Same as bacon; but it is usually so salty that it should be parboiled first, or soaked at least an hour in cold water.

Salt Pork, Boiled.—Nearly always cooked with vegetables or greens; hence need not be soaked or parboiled. See page 58.

Pork Fritters.—Make a thick batter of corn meal one-third and flour two-thirds, or of flour alone. Fry a few slices of pork until the fat is tried out. Then cut a few more slices, dip them in the batter, drop them in the bubbling fat, season with salt and pepper, fry to a light brown, and eat while hot. It takes the stomach of a lumberjack to digest this, but it is a favorite variant in frontier diet.

Pork and Hardtack.—Soak hardtack in water until it is partly softened. Drop it into hot pork fat, and cook. A soldier's resource.

Ham, Fried.—Same as bacon. Parboil, first, for eight or ten minutes, if hard and salty.

Ham and Eggs.—Same as bacon and eggs.

Ham, Broiled.—If salty, parboil first. Cut rather thick slices, pepper them, and broil five minutes. Ham that has been boiled is best for broiling. A little mustard may be spread on the slices when served.

Ham, Boiled.—Wash the ham, and let it soak over night in cold water. In the morning, cover it well with fresh water, bring to a boil, and hang the kettle high over the fire where it will boil gently until dinner time. When the bone on the under side leaves the meat readily, the ham is done. If you have eggs, the nicest way to serve a boiled ham is to remove the skin, brush over the top of ham with yolk of egg, sprinkle thickly with finely grated crumbs or cracker-dust, and brown in an oven.

Pork Sausages.—Cut links apart, prick each with a fork so it will not burst in cooking, lay in cold frying-pan, and fry fifteen to twenty minutes over a slow fire, moving them about so they will brown evenly all over. Serve with mashed potatoes, over which pour the fat from the pan. Apples fried to a light brown in the sausage grease are a pleasant accompaniment.

Corned Beef, Boiled.—Put the ham into enough cold water to cover it. Let it come slowly to a boil, and then merely simmer until done. Time, about one-half hour to each pound. Vegetables may be added toward the end, as directed on page 58. If not to be used until the next day, leave the meat in its liquor, weighted down under the surface by a clean rock.

Corned Beef Hash.—Chop some canned corned beef fine with sliced onions. Mash up with freshly boiled potatoes, two parts potatoes to one of meat. Season highly with pepper (no salt) and dry mustard if liked. Put a little pork fat in a frying-pan, melt, add hash, and cook until nearly dry and a brown crust has formed. Evaporated potatoes and onions can be used according to directions on packages.

Stew with Canned Meat.—Peel and slice some onions. If the meat has much fat, melt it; if not, melt a little pork fat. Add onions, and fry until brown. Mix some flour into a smooth batter with cold water, season with pepper and salt, and pour into the camp kettle. Stir the whole well together. Cut meat into slices, put into the kettle, and heat through.

Lobscouse.—Boil corned beef as above (if very salty, parboil first, and then change the water). About thirty minutes before it is done add sliced potatoes and hardtack.

Slumgullion.—When the commissariat is reduced to bacon, corned beef, and hardtack, try this sailor's dish, described by Jack London: Fry half a dozen slices of bacon, add fragments of hardtack, then two cups of water, and stir briskly over the fire; in a few minutes mix in with it slices of canned corned beef; season well with pepper and salt.

Dried Beef, Creamed.—Slice 3 oz. of dried beef into thin shavings. Pour over it a pint of boiling water, and let it stand two minutes. Turn off water, and drain beef dry. Heat a heaped tablespoonful of butter in the frying-pan; then add the beef. Cook three minutes, stirring all the time. Then pour on ¼ pint cold milk. Mix 4 tablespoonfuls milk with 1 teaspoonful flour, and stir into the beef in the pan. Cook two minutes longer and serve at once.

Canned Meats.—Never eat any that has been left standing open in the can. It is dangerous. If any has been left over, remove it to a clean vessel and keep in a cool place.

CURED FISH.

Salt Fish requires from twelve to thirty-six hours' soaking, flesh downward, in cold water before cooking, depending on the hardness and dryness of the fish. Change the water two or three times to remove surplus salt. Start in cold water, then, and boil until the flesh parts from the bones. When done, cover with bits of butter, or serve with one of the sauces given in the chapter on *Fish*.

Broiled Salt Fish.—Freshen the flakes of fish by soaking in cold water. Broil over the coals, and serve with potatoes.

Stewed Codfish.—Soak over night in plenty of cold water. Put in pot of fresh, cold water, and heat gradually until soft. Do not boil the fish or it will get hard. Serve with boiled potatoes, and with white sauce made as directed under *Fish*.

Codfish Hash.—Prepare salt codfish as above. When soft, mash with potatoes and onions, season with pepper, and fry like corned beef hash.

Codfish Balls.—Shred the fish into small pieces. Peel some potatoes. Use one pint of fish to one quart of raw potatoes. Put them in a pot, cover with boiling water, cook till potatoes are soft, drain water off, mash fish and potatoes together, and beat light with a fork. Add a tablespoonful of butter and season with pepper. Shape into flattened balls, and fry in very hot fat deep enough to cover.

Smoked Herrings.—(1) Clean, and remove the skin. Toast on a stick over the coals.

(2) Scald in boiling water till the skin curls up, then remove head, tail, and skin. Clean well. Put into frying-pan with a little butter or lard. Fry gently a few minutes, dropping in a little vinegar.

Smoked Sprats.—Lay them on a slightly greased plate and set them in an oven until heated through.

Canned Salmon, Creamed.—Cut into dice. Heat about a pint of them in one-half pint milk. Season with salt and Cayenne pepper. Cold cooked fish of any kind can be served in this way.

Canned Salmon, Scalloped.—Rub two teaspoonfuls of butter and a tablespoonful of flour together. Stir this into boiling milk. Cut two pounds of canned salmon into dice. Put a layer of the sauce in bottom of a dish, then a layer of salmon. Sprinkle with salt, Cayenne pepper, and grated bread crumbs. Repeat alternate layers until dish is full, having the last layer sauce, which is sprinkled with crumbs and bits of butter. Bake in very hot oven until browned (about ten minutes).

Canned Salmon on Toast.—Dip slices of stale bread in smoking-hot lard. They will brown at once. Drain them. Heat a pint of salmon, picked into flakes, season with salt and Cayenne, and turn into a cupful of melted butter. Heat in pan. Stir in one egg, beaten light, with three tablespoonfuls evaporated milk not thinned. Pour the mixture on the fried bread.

Sardines, Fried.—Fry them and give them a dash of red pepper. They are better if wiped free of oil, dipped into whipped egg, sprinkled thickly with cracker crumbs, fried, and served on buttered toast.

EGGS.

Desiccated Egg.—The baker's egg mentioned in my first chapter is in granules about the size of coarse sand. It is prepared for use by first soaking about two hours in cold or one hour in lukewarm water. Hot water must not be used. Solution can be quickened by occasional stirring. The proportion is one tablespoonful of egg to two of water, which is about the equivalent of one fresh egg. Use just like fresh eggs in baking, etc., and for scrambled eggs or omelets. Of course, the desiccated powder cannot be fried, boiled, or poached.

Fried Eggs.—Have the frying-pan scrupulously clean. Put in it just enough butter, dripping, or other fat, to prevent the eggs sticking. Break eggs separately in a cup, and drop them, one at a time, into the pan when it is hot. The fire should be moderate. As the eggs fry, raise their edges and ladle a little of the grease over the yolk. In two or three minutes they will be done. Eggs fried longer than this, or on both sides, are leathery and unwholesome.

Scrambled Eggs.—Put into a well-greased pan as many eggs as it will hold separately, each yolk being whole. When the whites have begun to set, stir from bottom of pan until done (buttery, not leathery). Add a piece of butter, pepper, and

salt. Another way is to beat the eggs with a
spoon. To eight eggs add one-third teaspoonful
salt. Heat two tablespoonfuls butter in the frying-pan. Stir in the eggs, and continue stirring
until eggs set. Before they toughen, turn them
out promptly into a warm dish.

Plain Omelet.—It is better to make two or
three small omelets than to attempt one large one.
Scrape the pan and wipe it dry after each omelet
is made. Use little salt: it keeps the eggs from
rising. Heat the fat in the pan very gradually,
but get it hot almost to the browning point.

Beat four eggs just enough to break them well.
Add one-half teaspoonful of salt. Put two heaped
teaspoonfuls of butter in the pan and heat as
above. Pour egg into pan, and tilt the pan forward so that the egg flows to the far side. As
soon as the egg begins to set, draw it up to the
raised side of the pan with a knife. Beginning
then at the left hand, turn the egg over in small
folds until the lower part of the pan is reached,
and the omelet has been rolled into a complete
fold. Let the omelet rest a few seconds, and
then turn out into a hot dish. Work rapidly
throughout, so that the omelet is creamy instead
of tough. It should be of a rich yellow color.

Ham Omelet.—Cut raw ham into dice. Fry.
Turn the beaten eggs over it and cook as above.
Bacon can be used instead of ham.

Fancy Omelets.—Take tender meat, game, fish,
or vegetable, hash it fine, heat it in white sauce
(see page 87), and spread this over the omelet
before you begin to fold it; or they can be put in
with the eggs. Jam, jelly, or preserved fruit may
be used in a similar way.

Rum Omelet.—Beat three eggs, add a very

small pinch of salt, a teaspoonful of powdered sugar, a slice of butter, and a tablespoonful of rum. Fry as described above. Lay the omelet on a hot dish, pour around it one-half tumblerful of rum that has been warmed in a pan, light it, and serve with its blue flame rising round it.

Poached Eggs.—Put a pint of water in the frying pan, with one-half teaspoonful of salt. If you have vinegar, add two teaspoonfuls to the water: it keeps the whites from running too much. Bring the water to a gentle boil. Break the eggs separately into a saucer and slide them into the water. Let the water simmer not longer than three minutes, meantime ladling spoonfuls of it over the yolks. Have toast already buttered on a very hot plate. Lay eggs carefully on it. Eat at once. This may be varied by moistening the toast with hot milk.

Eggs, Boiled.—Eggs are boiled soft in two and one-half to three minutes, depending upon size and freshness. If wanted hard boiled, put them in cold water, bring to a boil, and keep it up for twenty minutes. The yolk will then be mealy and wholesome. Eggs boiled between these extremes are either clammy or tough, and indigestible.

CHAPTER IX.

BREADSTUFFS AND CEREALS.

WHEN men must bake for themselves they generally make biscuit, biscuit-loaf, flapjacks, or corn bread. Bread leavened with yeast is either beyond their skill or too troublesome to make out of doors; so baking powder is the mainstay of the camp. Generally the batch is a failure. To paraphrase Tom Hood,

> Who has not met with camp-made bread,
> Rolled out of putty and weighted with lead?

It need not be so. Just as good biscuit or johnny cake can be baked before a log fire in the woods as in a kitchen range. Bread making is a chemical process. Follow directions; pay close attention to details, as a chemist does, from building the fire to testing the loaf with a sliver. It does require experience or a special knack to *guess* quantities accurately, but none at all to *measure* them.

In general, biscuit or other small cakes should be baked quickly by ardent heat; large loaves require a slow, even heat, so that the outside will not harden until the inside is nearly done.

The way to bake in a reflector or in a "baker" has been shown in the chapter on *Meats*. If you have neither of these utensils, there are other ways.

Baking in a Frying-pan.—Grease or flour a frying-pan and put a loaf in it. Rake some embers out in front of the fire and put pan on them just long enough to form a little crust on bottom of loaf. Then remove from embers, and, with a short forked stick, the stub of which will enter hole in end of handle, prop pan up before fire at such angle that top of loaf will be exposed to heat. Turn loaf now and then, both sidewise and upside down. When firm enough to keep its shape, remove it, prop it by itself before the fire to finish baking, and go on with a fresh loaf. A tin plate may be used in place of the frying-pan.

Baking on a Slab.—Heat a thick slab of non-resinous green wood until the sap simmers. Then proceed as with a frying-pan.

Baking on a Stick.—Work dough into a ribbon two inches wide. Get a club of sweet green wood (birch, sassafras, maple), about two feet long and three inches thick, peel large end, sharpen the other and stick it into ground, leaning toward fire. When sap simmers wind dough spirally around peeled end. Turn occasionally. Several sticks can be baking at once. Bread for one man's meal can be quickly baked on a peeled stick as thick as a broomstick, holding over fire and turning.

Baking in the Ashes.—Build a good fire on a level bit of ground. When it has burned to coals and the ground has thoroughly heated, rake away the embers, lightly drop the loaf on the hot earth, pat it smooth, rake the embers back over the loaf, and let it bake until no dough will adhere to a sliver thrust to the center of the loaf. This is the Australian damper. Ash cakes are

similarly baked (see under *Corn Bread*). Nasty?
No, it isn't; try it.

Baking in a Hole.—Every fixed camp should
have a bake-hole, if for nothing else than baking
beans. The hole can be dug anywhere, but it is
best in the side of a bank or knoll, so that an
opening can be left in front to rake out of, and
for drainage in case of rain. Line it with stones,
if there are any. In any case, have the completed
hole a little larger than your baking kettle.

Build a hardwood fire in and above the hole
and keep it going until the stones or earth are very
hot (not less than half an hour). Rake out most
of the coals and ashes, put in the bake-pot, which
must have a tight-fitting lid, cover with ashes and
then with live coals; and, if a long heating is
needed, keep a small fire going on top. Close
the mouth of the oven with a flat rock. This is
the way for beans or for braising meat.

Bread is not easily baked in a straight-sided
pot (rather it is hard to get out when baked).
A pan with flaring sides, well covered, is better. Two pudding pans that nest, the larger inverted over the smaller, do very well. Have some
ashes between them and the coals, to prevent
burning the loaf.

A shifty camper can bake bread in almost
anything. I have baked beans in a thin, soldered,
lard-pail, by first encasing it in clay.

Baking in a Dutch Oven.—This is a cast-iron
pot with flaring sides and short legs, fitted with
a thick iron cover, the rim of which is turned
up to hold a layer of coals on top. If it were
not for its weight it would be the best oven for
outdoor use, since it not only bakes but cooks
the meat or pone in its own steam. The pots

made for fireless cookers can be used in a similar way.

Place the Dutch oven and its lid separately on the fire. Get the bottom moderately hot, and the lid very hot (but not red, lest it warp). Grease the bottom and sprinkle flour over it, put in the bread or biscuits, set cover on, rake a thin layer of coals out in front of the fire, stand oven on them, and cover lid thickly with more live coals. Replenish occasionally. Have a stout pot-hook to lift lid with, so you can inspect progress of baking, once or twice.

WHEAT BREAD AND BISCUITS.

When baking powder is used, the secret of good bread is to *handle the dough as little as possible.* After adding the water, mix as rapidly as you can, not with the warm hands, but with a big spoon or a wooden paddle. To knead such bread, or roll it much, or even to mould biscuits by hand instead of cutting them out, would surely make your baking "sad." As soon as water touches the flour, the baking powder begins to give off gas. It is this gas, imprisoned in the dough, that makes bread light. Squeezing or moulding presses this gas out. The heat of the hands turns such dough into Tom Hood's "putty."

Biscuit Loaf.—This is a standard camp bread, because it bakes quickly. It is good so long as it is hot, but it dries out soon and will not keep. For four men:

> 3 pints flour,
> 3 heaping teaspoonfuls baking powder,
> 1 heaping teaspoonful salt,
> 2 heaping tablespoonfuls cold grease,
> 1 scant pint cold water.

Amount of water varies according to quality of

flour. Baking powders vary in strength; follow directions on can.

Mix thoroughly, with big spoon or wooden paddle, first the baking powder with the flour, and then the salt. Rub into this the cold grease (which may be lard, cold pork fat, drippings, or bear's grease), until there are no lumps left and no grease adhering to bottom of pan. This is a little tedious, but don't shirk it. Then stir in the water and work it with spoon until you have a rather stiff dough. Have the pan greased. Turn the loaf into it, and bake. Test center of loaf with a sliver when you think it probably done. When no dough adheres, remove bread. All hot breads should be broken with the hands, never cut.

To freshen any that is left over and dried out, sprinkle a little water over it and heat through. This can be done but once.

Biscuit.—These are baked in a reflector (12-inch holds 1 dozen, 18-inch holds 1½ dozen), unless a camp stove is carried or an oven is dug. Build the fire high. Make dough as in the preceding recipe, which is enough for two dozen biscuits. Flop the mass of dough to one side of pan, dust flour on bottom of pan, flop dough back over it, dust flour on top of loaf. Now rub some flour over the bread board, flour your hands, and gently lift loaf on board. Flour the bottle or bit of peeled sapling that you use as rolling-pin, also the edges of can or can cover used as biscuit cutter. Gently roll loaf to three-quarter-inch thickness. Stamp out the biscuit and lay them in pan. Roll out the culls and make biscuit of them, too. Bake until edge of front row turns brown; reverse pan and continue until rear row is simi-

larly done. Time, twenty to twenty-five minutes in a reflector, ten to fifteen minutes in a closed
oven.

Dropped Biscuit.—These do away with bread-
board, rolling-pin, and most of the work, yet are
about as good as stamped biscuit. Use same
proportions as above, except turn in enough water
to make a *thick batter*—one that will drop lazily
from a spoon. In mixing, do not stir the batter
more than necessary to smooth out all lumps.
Drop from a big spoon into the greased bake-pan.

Army Bread.—This is easier to make than biscuit dough, since there is no grease to rub in, but
it takes longer to bake. It keeps fresh longer
than yeast bread, does not dry up in a week, nor
mould, and is more wholesome than biscuit. It
is the only baking-powder bread I know of that is
good to eat cold—in fact, it is best that way.

    1 quart flour,
    1 teaspoonful salt,
    1 tablespoonful sugar,
    2 heaped teaspoonfuls baking powder.

Mix the dry ingredients thoroughly. Then stir
in enough cold water (about 1½ pints) to make a
thick batter that will pour out level. Mix rapidly with spoon until smooth, and pour at once
into bake-pan. Bake about forty-five minutes, or
until no dough adheres to a sliver. Above quantity makes a 1½-pound loaf (say 9x5x3 inches).

Breakfast Rolls.—

    1 quart flour,
    2 level tablespoonfuls butter,
    1 egg,
    1 teaspoonful baking powder,
    1 pint cold milk (or enough to make a soft dough).

Rub butter and flour well together, add beaten
egg, a pinch of salt, and the milk, till a soft dough
is mixed. Form into rolls and bake quickly.

Sour-dough Bread.—Mix a pail of batter from plain flour and water, and hang it up in a warm place until the batter sours. Then add salt and soda (not baking powder), thicken with flour to a stiff dough, knead thoroughly, work into small loaves, and place them before the fire to rise. Then bake.

Salt-rising Bread.—This smells to heaven while it is fermenting, but is a welcome change after a long diet of baking-powder breadstuffs. For a baking of two or three loaves take about a pint of moderately warm water (a pleasant heat to the hand) and stir into it as much flour as will make a good batter, not too thick. Add to this one-half teaspoonful salt, not more. Set the vessel in a pan of moderately warm water, within a little distance of a fire, or in sunlight. The water must not be allowed to cool much below the original heat, more warm water being added to pan as required.

In six to eight hours the whole will be in active fermentation, when the dough must be mixed with it, and as much warm water (milk, if you have it) as you require. Knead the mass till it is tough and does not stick to the board. Make up your loaves, and keep them warmly covered near the fire till they rise. They must be baked as soon as this second rising takes place; for, unless the rising is used immediately on reaching its height, it sinks to rise no more.

To Raise Bread in a Pot.—Set the dough to rise over a very few embers, keeping the pot turned as the loaf rises. When equally risen all around, put hot ashes under the pot and upon the lid, taking care that the heat be not too fierce at first.

Lungwort Bread.—On the bark of maples, and sometimes of beeches and birches, in the northern woods, there grows a green, broad-leaved lichen variously known as lungwort, liverwort, lung-lichen, and lung-moss, which is an excellent substitute for yeast.. This is an altogether different growth from the plants commonly called lung-wort and liverwort—I believe its scientific name is *Sticta pulmonacea.* This lichen is partly made up of fungus, which does the business of raising dough. Gather a little of it and steep it over night in lukewarm water, set near the embers, but not near enough to get overheated. In the morning, pour off the infusion and mix it with enough flour to make a batter, beating it up with a spoon. Place this "sponge" in a warm can or pail, cover with a cloth, and set it near the fire to work. By evening it will have risen. Leaven your dough with this (saving some of the sponge for a future baking), let the bread rise before the fire that night, and by morning it will be ready to bake.

It takes but little of the original sponge to leaven a large mass of dough (but see that it never freezes), and it can be kept good for months.

Unleavened Bread.—Quickly made, wholesome, and good for a change. Keeps like hardtack.

> 2½ pints flour,
> 1 tablespoonful salt,
> 1 tablespoonful sugar.

Mix with water to stiff dough, and knead and pull until lively. Roll out thin as a soda cracker, score with knife, and bake. Unleavened bread that is to be carried for a long time must be mixed with as little water as possible (merely dampened enough to make it adhere), for if any moisture is left in it after baking, it will mould.

To Mix Dough Without a Pan.—When bark
will peel, use a broad sheet of it (paper birch,
basswood, poplar, cottonwood, slippery elm, etc.).
It is easy to mix unleavened dough in the sack
of flour itself. Stand the latter horizontally where
it can't fall over. Scoop a bowl-shaped depression in top of flour. Keep the right hand moving
round while you pour in a little water at a time
from a vessel held in the left. Sprinkle a little
salt in. When a thick, adhesive dough has formed,
lift this out and pat and work it into a round
cake about 2½ inches thick.

CORN BREAD.

Plain corn bread, without flour, milk, or egg,
is hard to make eatable without a Dutch oven to
bake it in. Even so, it is generally spoiled by being baked too fast and not long enough to be done
inside.

Johnny Cake.—
    1 quart meal,
    1 teaspoonful salt,
    1 pint *warm* (but not scalding) water (1½ pints
       for old meal).

Stir together until light. Bake to a nice brown
all around (about forty-five minutes), and let it
sweat fifteen minutes longer in the closed oven,
removed from the fire. Yellow meal generally
requires more water than white. Freshly ground
meal is much better than old.

Corn Dodgers.—Same as above, but mix to a
stiff dough, and form into cylindrical dodgers four
or five inches long and 1½ inches diameter, by
rolling between the hands. Have frying-pan very
hot, grease it a little, and put dodgers on as you
roll them out. As soon as they have browned, put
them in oven and bake thoroughly.

Ash Cake.—Same kind of dough. Form it into balls as big as hen's eggs, roll in dry flour, lay in hot ashes, and cover completely with them.

Corn Bread (Superior).—

> 1 pint corn meal,
> 1 pint flour,
> 3 tablespoonfuls sugar,
> 2 heaped tablespoonfuls butter,
> 3 teaspoonfuls baking powder,
> 1 teaspoonful salt,
> 2 eggs,
> 1 pint (or more) milk.

Rub butter and sugar together. Add the beaten eggs; then the milk. Sift the salt and baking powder into the meal and flour. Pour the liquid over the dry ingredients, beating well. Pour batter into well-greased pan, and bake thirty to forty minutes in moderately hot oven. Can also be made into muffins.

Corn Batter Bread.—

> 1 pint corn meal,
> 2 pints milk (or water),
> 2 eggs,
> 1 teaspoonful salt.

Beat the eggs light; add the salt; then the meal and milk, gradually, until well blended. Bake about thirty minutes. This is the standard breakfast bread of the South, easily made, and (if the meal is freshly ground) delicious. A little boiled rice, or hominy grits, may be substituted for part of the meal.

Snow Bread.—After a fall of light, feathery snow, superior corn bread may be made by stirring together

> 1 quart corn meal,
> ½ teaspoonful soda,
> 1 teaspoonful salt,
> 1 tablespoonful lard.

Then, in a cool place where snow will not melt, stir into above one quart light snow. Bake about forty minutes in rather hot oven. Snow, for some unknown reason, has the same effect on bread as eggs have, two tablespoonfuls of snow equaling one egg. It can also be used in making batter for pancakes, or puddings, the batter being made rather thick, and the snow mixed with each cake just before putting in the pan.

Substitute for Baking Soda.—Take the *white* of wood ashes, same quantity as you would use of soda, and mix dry with the flour. It makes bread rise the same as soda, and you can't tell the difference. The best ashes are those of hickory, dogwood, sugar maple, and corncobs; beech, ash, buckeye, balsam poplar, and yellow poplar are also good.

"Gritted Bread."—When green corn has become too hard for boiling, but is still too soft for grinding into meal, make a "gritter," as follows: Take a piece of tin about 7 x 14 inches (unsolder a lard pail by heating, and flatten the sides); punch holes through it, close together, with a large nail; bend the sheet into a half cylinder, rough side out, like a horseradish grater; nail the edges to a board somewhat longer and wider than the tin. Then, holding the ear of corn pointing lengthwise from you, grate it into a vessel held between the knees.

The meal thus formed will need no water, but can be mixed in its own milk. Salt it, and bake quickly. The flavor of "gritted bread" is a blend of hot pone and roasting ears—delectable! Hard corn can be grated by first soaking the ears over night.

Plain Flapjacks.—

- 1 quart flour,
- 1 teaspoonful salt,
- 2 teaspoonfuls sugar, or 4 of molasses,
- 2 level tablespoonfuls baking powder.

Rub in, dry, two heaped tablespoonfuls grease. If you have no grease, do without. Make a smooth batter with cold milk (best) or water—thin enough to pour from a spoon, but not too thin, or it will take all day to bake enough for the party. Stir well, to smooth out lumps. Set frying-pan level over thin bed of coals, get it quite hot, and grease with a piece of pork in split end of stick. Pan must be hot enough to make batter sizzle as it touches, and it should be polished. Pour from end of a big spoon successively enough batter to fill pan within one-half inch of rim. When cake is full of bubbles and edges have stiffened, shuffle pan to make sure that cake is free below and stiff enough to flip. Then hold pan slanting in front of and away from you, go through preliminary motion of flapping once or twice to get the swing, then flip boldly so cake will turn a somersault in the air, and catch it upside down. Beginners generally lack the nerve to toss high enough. Grease pan anew and stir batter every time before pouring. This is the "universal pancake" that Nessmuk derided. Much better and wholesomer are:

Egg Pancakes.—Made same as above excepting that you add two eggs, or their equivalent in desiccated egg.

Snow Pancakes.—Instead of eggs, in the above recipe, use four tablespoonfuls of freshly fallen snow. Make the batter rather thick, and add

some clean, dry snow to each pancake before putting it in the pan.

Mixed Cakes.—When cold boiled rice is left
over, mix it half and half with flour, and proceed
as with flapjacks. The batter is best mixed with
the water in which the rice was boiled. Oatmeal,
grits, or cold boiled potatoes, may be used in the
same way.

Corn Batter Cakes.—

    ½ pint corn meal,
    ¼ pint flour,
    1 heaped teaspoonful baking powder,
    1 heaped teaspoonful sugar or 2 molasses,
    1 level teaspoonful salt,

After mixing the dry ingredients thoroughly,
add cold water, a little at a time, stirring briskly,
until a rather thick batter results. Bake like flapjacks. Wholesomer than plain flour flapjacks.
These are better with an egg or two added, and
if mixed with milk instead of water. Snow can be
substituted for eggs, as described above.

Buckwheat Cakes.—

    1 pint buckwheat flour,
    ½ pint wheat flour,
    2 tablespoonfuls baking powder,
    ½ teaspoonful salt.

Mix to a thin batter, preferably with milk. A
couple of eggs make them light, or, make snow
cakes.

TOAST, FRITTERS, DUMPLINGS, ETC.

Stale Bread.—Biscuit or bread left over and
dried out can be freshened for an hour or two by
dipping quickly in and out of water and placing
in the baker until heated through; or, the biscuit
may be cut open, slightly moistened, and toasted
in a broiler.

If you have eggs, make a French toast by dipping the slices in whipped eggs and frying them. With milk, make milk toast: heat the milk, add a chunk of butter and some salt, toast the bread, and pour milk over it.

Stale bread may also be dipped into smoking hot grease. It will brown immediately. Stand it edgewise to drain, then lay on hot plate. Cut into dice for soups.

Fried Quoits.—Make dough as for biscuit. Plant a stick slanting in the ground near the fire. Have another small, clean stick ready, and a frying-pan of lard or butter heated sissing hot. There must be enough grease in the pan to drown the quoits. Take dough the size of a small hen's egg, flatten it between the hands, make a hole in the center like that of a doughnut, and quickly work it (the dough, not the hole) into a flat ring of about two inches inside diameter. Drop it flat into the hot grease, turn almost immediately, and in a few seconds it will be cooked.

When of a light brown color, fish it out with your little stick and hang it on the slanting one before the fire to keep hot. If the grease is of the right temperature, the cooking of one quoit will occupy just the same time as the molding of another, and the product will be crisp and crumpety. If the grease is not hot enough, a visit from your oldest grandmother may be expected before midnight. (Adapted from *Lees and Clutterbuck.*)

Fritters.—A dainty variety is added to the camp bill-of-fare by fritters of fruit or vegetables, fish, flesh, or fowl. They are especially relished in cold weather, or when the butter supply is low. Being easily made and quickly cooked, they fit any time or place.

The one essential of good and wholesome fritters is plenty of fat to fry them in, and fat of
the right temperature. (The best friture is equal
parts of butter and lard.) Set the kettle where
the fat will heat slowly until needed; then closer
over the fire until a bluish smoke rises from the
center of the kettle. Drop a cube of bread into
it; if it turns golden-brown in one minute, the fat
is right. Then keep the kettle at just this temperature. Make batter as follows:

Fritter Batter.—
    1 pint flour,
    4 eggs,
    1 tablespoonful salt,
    1 pint water or milk,
    3 tablespoonfuls butter or other grease.

Blend the salt and the yolks of the eggs (or
desiccated egg). Rub the butter into this; then
the flour, a little at a time; then the water. Beat
well, and, if you have time, let it stand a while.
If fresh eggs are used, now beat the whites to a
stiff froth and stir them in. When using, drop
even spoonfuls into the fat with a large spoon.
When golden-brown, lift fritter out with a forked
stick (not piercing), stand it up to drain, and
serve very hot. The base may be almost anything: sliced fruit, minced game or meat, fish or
shellfish, grated cheese, boiled rice, grated potato
or green corn, etc. Anything cut to the size of
an oyster is dipped in the batter and then fried;
if minced or grated it is mixed with the batter.
Jam is spread on bread, covered with another
slice, the sandwich is cut into convenient pieces,
and these are dipped in the batter. Plain fritters .
of batter alone are eaten with syrup. Those
made of corn meal instead of flour (mixed with
warm milk and egg) are particularly good. The

variety that can be served, even in camp, is well-nigh endless.

Dumplings.—Those of biscuit dough have already been mentioned. When specially prepared they may be made as follows:

½ pint flour,
1 teaspoonful baking powder,
¼ teaspoonful salt,
½ teaspoonful sugar,
⅙ pint milk.

The stew that they are to be cooked with should be nearly done before the dumplings are started. Then mix the dry ingredients thoroughly. Wet with the milk and stir quickly into a smooth ball. Roll into a sheet three-quarters of an inch thick, and cut like biscuit. Meantime bring the stew to a sharp boil. Arrange dumplings on top of it, cover the vessel, and cook exactly ten minutes.

MACARONI.

Boiled Macaroni.—For one-half pound macaroni have not less than three quarts of salted water boiling rapidly. Break the macaroni into short pieces, and boil thirty-five minutes for the small, forty-five minutes for the large. Then drain, and pour sauce over it, or bake it. It is better if boiled in good broth instead of water.

Tomato Sauce.—

1 quart can tomatoes,
1 tablespoonful butter,
2 tablespoonfuls flour,
1 teaspoonful salt,
⅛ teaspoonful pepper,
1 teaspoonful sugar.

Rub the flour into the butter until they blend. Brown this in a pan. Add the tomatoes and simmer thirty minutes. Stir frequently. Add the seasoning, along with spices, if you wish. This makes enough sauce for 1½ pounds macaroni, but it keeps well in cold weather, and can be used with other dishes. Good in combination with the following:

Macaroni with Cheese.—After the macaroni is boiled, put it in a pan with a little butter and some grated cheese. Stir gently, and as soon as the cheese is melted, serve; or, pour the above sauce over it.

Macaroni, Baked.—Boil first, as above. Drain. Place in a deep pan, add a cupful of cold milk, sprinkle in three tablespoonfuls grated cheese and one tablespoonful butter. Then bake until brown.

PORRIDGE.

Corn Meal Mush.—Mix two level tablespoonfuls salt with one quart meal. Bring four quarts of water (for yellow meal, or half as much for fresh white meal) to a hard boil in a two-gallon kettle. Mix the salted meal with enough *cold* water to make a batter that will run from the spoon; this is to prevent it from getting lumpy. With a large spoon drop the batter into the boiling water, adding gradually, so that water will not fall below boiling point. Stir constantly for ten minutes. Then cover pot and hang it high enough above fire to insure against scorching. Cook thus for one hour, stirring occasionally, and thinning with *boiling* water if it gets too thick.

Fried Mush.—This, as Father Izaak said of another dish, is "too good for any but very honest men." The only drawback to this gastronomic joy is that it takes a whole panful for one man. As it is rather slow to fry, let each man perform over the fire for himself. The mush should have been poured into a greased pan the previous evening, and set in a cool place over night to harden. Cut into slices one-third of an inch thick, and fry in very hot grease until nicely browned. Eat with syrup, or *au naturel*.

Polenta.—An Italian dish made from our native corn and decidedly superior to plain boiled mush. Cook mush as above for one hour. Partly fill the bake-pan with it, and pour over it either a good brown gravy, or the tomato sauce described under macaroni. Then sprinkle with grated cheese. Set the pan in the oven three minutes, or in the reflector five minutes, to bake a little.

Oatmeal Porridge.—Rolled oats may be cooked much more quickly than the old-fashioned oatmeal; the latter is not fit for the human stomach until it has been boiled as long as corn mush. To two quarts boiling water add one teaspoonful of salt, stir in gradually a pint of rolled oats, and boil ten minutes, stirring constantly, unless you have a double boiler. The latter may be extemporized by setting a small kettle inside a larger one that contains some water.

CEREALS.

Rice, Boiled.—Good precedent to the contrary notwithstanding, I contend that there is but one way to boil rice, and that is this (which is described in the words of Captain Kenealy, whose *Yachting Wrinkles* is a book worth owning):

To cook rice so that each grain will be plump, dry, and separate, first, wash the measure of rice thoroughly in cold, salted water. Then put it in a pot of *furiously boiling* fresh water, no salt being added. Keep the pot boiling hard for twenty minutes, but *do not stir*. Then strain off the water, place the rice over a very moderate fire (hang high over camp-fire), and let it swell and dry for half an hour, in an uncovered vessel. Remember that rice swells enormously in cooking.

Rice, Fried.—When boiled rice is left over, spread it in a dish. When cold, cut it into cakes and fry it, for a hasty meal. It is better, though, in muffins.

Rice Muffins.—Mash very smooth half a pint boiled rice. Add slowly, stirring to a thinner paste, half a pint of milk, three beaten eggs, salt. Then make into a stiff batter with flour. Bake like dropped biscuits.

Risotto.—Fry a sliced onion brown in a tablespoonful of butter. Add to this a pint of hot water and half a pint of washed rice. Boil until soft, adding more hot water if needed. Heat half a pint canned tomatoes, and stir into it a teaspoonful of sugar. When the rice is soft, salt it; add the tomato; turn into a dish and sprinkle over it a heaped tablespoonful of grated cheese.

Rice, Curried.—Same as Risotto, but put a teaspoonful of curry powder in the tomatoes and omit cheese.

Grits, Boiled.—Put in plenty of boiling unsalted water. Boil about thirty minutes; then salt and drain.

Grits, Fried.—Same as fried rice.

"Breakfast Foods."—According to directions on packages.

Left-over Cereals.—See Mixed Cakes, page 114.

CHAPTER X.

VEGETABLES.—SOUPS.

FRESH *Vegetables.*—Do not wash them until just before they are to be cooked or eaten. They lose flavor quickly after being washed. This is true even of potatoes.

Fresh vegetables go into plenty of fast-boiling salted water. Salt prevents their absorbing too much water. The water should be boiling fast, and there should be plenty of it. They should be boiled rapidly, with the lid left off the pan. If the water is as hot as it should be, the effect is similar to that which we have noted in the case of meats: the surface is coagulated into a waterproof envelope which seals up the flavor instead of letting it be soaked out. In making soup, the rule is reversed.

Dried Vegetables.—Beans and peas are to be cooked in unsalted water. If salted too soon they become leathery and difficult to cook. Put them in cold, fresh water, gradually heated to the boiling point, and boil slowly.

Desiccated (dehydrated) Vegetables.—Follow directions on package. Desiccated potatoes of the ordinary kind require long soaking in cold water. Then put them in water slightly salted and proceed as with fresh potatoes. They may need boiling in three waters.

Canned Vegetables.—The liquor of canned peas,

121

string beans, etc., is unfit for use and should be thrown away; this does not apply to tomatoes.

Cleaning Vegetables.—To clear cabbage, etc., from insects, immerse them, stalk upward, in plenty of cold water salted in the proportion of a large tablespoonful to two quarts. Vinegar may be used instead of salt. Shake occasionally. The insects will sink to bottom of pan.

Storing Vegetables.—To keep vegetables, put them in a cool, dry place (conditions similar to those of a good cellar). Keep each kind away from the other, or they will absorb each other's flavor.

Potatoes, Boiled.—Pick them out as nearly as possible of one size, or some will boil to pieces before the others are done; if necessary, cut them to one size. Remove eyes and specks, and pare as thinly as possible, for the best of the potato lies just under the skin. As fast as pared, throw into cold water, and leave until wanted. Put in furiously boiling salted water, then hang kettle a little higher where it will boil moderately, but do not let it check. Test with a fork or sliver. When the tubers are done (about twenty minutes for new potatoes, thirty to forty minutes for old ones) drain off all the water, dust some salt over the potatoes (it absorbs the surface moisture), and let the pot stand uncovered close to the fire, shaking it gently once or twice, till the surface of each potato is dry and powdery. Never leave potatoes in the water after they are done; they become watery.

Potatoes, Boiled in Their Jackets.—After washing thoroughly, and gouging out the eyes, snip off a bit from each end of the potato; this gives a vent to the steam and keeps potatoes from bursting open. I prefer to put them in cold water and bring it gradually to a boil, because the skin of the potato contains an acid poison which is thus extracted. The water in which potatoes have been boiled will poison a dog. Of course we don't "eat 'em skin and all," like the people in the nursery rhyme; but there is no use in driving the bitterness into a potato. Boil gently, but continuously, throw in a little salt now and then, drain, and dry before the fire.

Potatoes, Steamed.—Old potatoes are better steamed. A rough-and-ready method is shown on page 60.

Potatoes, Mashed.—After boiling, mash the potatoes with a peeled stub of sapling, or a bottle, and work into them some butter, if you have it, and milk. "The more you beat 'em, the better they be." Salt and pepper.

Potato Cakes.—Mould some mashed potato into cakes, season, and fry in deep fat. Or add egg and bake them brown.

Potatoes, Baked.—Nessmuk's description cannot be improved: "Scoop out a basin-like depression under the fore-stick, three or four inches deep, and large enough to hold the tubers when laid side by side; fill it with bright hardwood coals and keep up a strong heat for half an hour or more. Next, clean out the hollow, place the potatoes in it, and cover them with hot sand or ashes, topped with a heap of glowing coals, and keep up all the heat you like. In about forty minutes commence to try them with a sharpened hardwood sliver; when this will pass through them they are done and should be raked out at once. Run the sliver through them from end to end, to let the steam escape, and use immediately, as a roast potato quickly becomes soggy and bitter."

Potatoes, Fried.—Boiled or steamed potatoes that have been left over may be sliced one-quarter inch thick, and fried.

Potatoes, Fried, Raw.—Peel, and slice into pieces half an inch thick. Drop into cold water until frying-pan is ready. Put enough grease in pan to completely immerse the potatoes, and get it very hot, as directed under Frying. Pour water off potatoes, dry a slice in a clean cloth, drop it into the sizzling fat, and so on, one slice at a time. Drying the slices avoids a splutter in the pan and helps to keep from absorbing grease. If many slices were dropped into the pan together, the heat would be checked and the potatoes would get soggy with grease. When the slices begin to turn a faint brown, salt the potatoes, pour off the grease at once, and brown a little in the dry pan. The outside of each slice will then be crisp and the insides white and deliciously mealy.

Potatoes, Lyonnaise.—Fry one or more sliced onions until they are turning yellowish, then add sliced potatoes, previously boiled or steamed; keep tossing now and then until the potatoes are fried somewhat yellow; salt to taste.

Potatoes, Stewed.—Cut cold boiled potatoes into dice, season with salt, pepper, butter, and stew gently in enough milk to cover them. Stir occasionally to prevent scorching. Or peel and slice some raw potatoes. Cover with boiling water and boil until tender. Pour off the water. Roll a large piece of butter in flour, heat some milk, beat these together until smooth, season with salt and pepper, and bring to a boil. Then stew together five minutes. Serve very hot.

Sweet Potatoes, Boiled.—Use a kettle with lid. Select tubers of uniform size; wash; do not cut or break the skins. Put them in boiling water, and continue boiling until, when you pierce one with a fork, you find it just a little hard in the center. Drain by raising the cover only a trifle when kettle is tilted, so as to keep in as much steam as possible. Hang the kettle high over the fire, cover closely, and let steam ten minutes.

Sweet Potatoes, Fried.—Skin the boiled potatoes and cut them lengthwise. Dust the slices with salt and pepper. Throw them into hot fat, browning first one side, then the other. Serve very hot.

Potatoes and Onions, Hashed.—Slice two potatoes to one onion. Parboil together about fifteen minutes in salted water. Pour off water, and drain. Meantime be frying some bacon. When it is done, remove it to a hot side dish, turn the vegetables into the pan, and fry them to a light brown. Then fall to, and enjoy a good thing!

Beans, Boiled.—Pick out all defective beans, and wash the rest. It is best to soak the beans over night; but if time does not permit, add one-quarter teaspoonful of baking soda to the parboiling water. In either case, start in fresh cold water, and parboil one quart of beans (for four men with hearty appetites) for one-half hour, or until one will pop open when blown upon. At the same time parboil separately one pound fat salt pork. Remove scum from beans as it rises. Drain both; place beans around the pork, add two quarts boiling water, and boil slowly for two hours, or until tender. Drain, and season with salt and pepper.

It does not hurt beans to boil all day, provided boiling water is added from time to time, lest they get dry and scorch. The longer they boil the more digestible they become.

Beans, Baked.—Soak and parboil, as above, both the beans and the pork. Then pour off the water from the pork, gash the meat with a knife, spread half of it over the bottom of the kettle, drain the beans, pour them into the kettle, put the rest of pork on top, sprinkle not more than one-half teaspoonful of salt over the beans, pepper liberally, and if you have molasses, pour a tablespoonful over all; otherwise a tablespoonful of sugar. Hang the kettle high over the fire where it will not scorch, and bake at least two hours; or, add enough boiling water to just cover the beans, place kettle in bake-hole as directed on page 56, and bake all night, being careful that there are not enough embers with the ashes to burn the beans.

Baked beans are strong food, ideal for active men in cold weather. One can work harder and longer on pork and beans, without feeling hungry, than on any other food with which I am acquainted, save bear meat. The ingredients are compact and easy to transport; they keep indefinitely in any weather. But when one is only beginning camp life he should be careful not to overload his stomach with beans, for they are rather indigestible until you have toned up your stomach by hearty exercise in the open air.

Onions, Boiled.—More wholesome this way than fried or baked. Like potatoes, they should be of as uniform size as possible, for boiling. Do not boil them in an iron vessel. Put them in enough boiling salted water to cover them. Cover the kettle and boil gently, lest the onions break. They are cooked when a straw will pierce them (about an hour). If you wish them mild, boil in two or three waters. When cooked, drain and season with butter or dripping, pepper, and salt. Boiled milk, thickened, is a good sauce.

Green Corn.—If you happen to camp near a farm in the "roasting-ear" season, you are in great luck. The quickest way to roast an ear of corn is to cut off the butt of the ear closely, so that the pith of the cob is exposed, ream it out a little, impale the cob lengthwise on the end of a long hardwood stick, and turn over the coals.

To bake in the ashes: remove one outer husk, stripping off the silk, break off about an inch of the silk end, and twist end of husks tightly down over the broken end. Then bake in the ashes and embers as directed for potatoes. Time, about one hour.

To boil: prepare as above, but tie the ends of husks; this preserves the sweetness of the corn. Put in enough boiling salted water to cover the ears. Boil thirty minutes. Like potatoes, corn is injured by over-boiling. When cooked, cut off the butt and remove the shucks.

Cold boiled corn may be cut from the cob and fried, or mixed with mashed potatoes and fried.

Greens.—One who camps early in the season can add a toothsome dish, now and then, to his menu by gathering fresh greens in the woods and marshes.*

As a salad (watercress, peppergrass, dandelion, wild mustard, sorrel, etc.): wash in cold salted water, if necessary, although this abstracts some of the flavor; dry immediately and thoroughly.

---

*Nearly a hundred edible wild plants, besides mushrooms and fruits, are discussed in my *Camping and Woodcraft,* Chap. XVII.

Break into convenient pieces, rejecting tough stems. Prepare a simple French dressing, thus:

1 tablespoonful vinegar,
3 tablespoonfuls best olive oil,
½ teaspoonful salt,
¼ teaspoonful black pepper.

Put salt and pepper in bowl, gradually add oil, rubbing and mixing till salt is dissolved; then add by degrees the vinegar, stirring continuously one minute. In default of oil, use cream and melted butter; but plain vinegar, salt, and pepper will do. Pour the dressing over the salad, turn the latter upside down, mix well, and serve.

A scalded salad is prepared in camp by cutting bacon into small dice, frying, adding vinegar, pepper, and a little salt to the grease, and pouring this, scalding hot, over the greens.

Greens may be boiled with salt pork, bacon, or other meat. To boil them separately: first soak in cold salted water for a few minutes, then drain well, and put into enough boiling salted water to cover, pressing them down until the pot is full. Cover, and boil steadily until tender, which may be from twenty minutes to an hour, depending upon kind of greens used. If the plants are a little older than they should be, parboil in water to which a little baking soda has been added; then drain, and continue boiling in plain water, salted.

Some greens are improved by chopping fine after boiling, putting in hot frying-pan with a tablespoonful of butter and some salt and pepper, and stirring until thoroughly heated.

Poke stalks are cooked like asparagus. They should not be over four inches long, and should show only a tuft of leaves at the top; if much older than this, they are unwholesome. Wash the stalks, scrape them, and lay in cold water for an hour; then tie loosely in bundles, put in a kettle of boiling water, and boil three-fourths of an hour, or until tender; drain, lay on buttered toast, dust with pepper and salt, cover with melted butter, and serve.

Jerusalem artichokes must be watched when boiling and removed as soon as tender; if left longer in the water they harden.

Dock and sorrel may be cooked like spinach: pick over and wash, drain, shake, and press out adhering water; put in kettle with one cup water, cover kettle, place over moderate fire, and steam thus twenty minutes; then drain, chop very fine, and heat in frying-pan as directed above.

Mushrooms.—Every one who camps in summer should take with him a mushroom book, such as Gibson's, Atkinson's, or Nina Marshall's. (Such a book in pocket form, with *colored* illustrations, is a desideratum.) Follow recipes in book. Mushrooms are very easy to prepare, cook quickly, and offer a great variety of flavors.

All mushrooms on the following list are delicious:

Coprinus comatus.	*Lactarius volemus.*
Hypholoma appendiculatum.	" *deliciosus.*
Tricholoma personatum.	*Russula alutacea.*
Boletus subaureus.	" *virescens.*
" *bovinus.*	*Cantharellus cibarius.*
" *subsanguineous.*	*Marasmius oreades.*
Clavaria botrytes.	*Hydnum repandum.*
" *cinerea.*	" *Caput-Medusæ.*
" *vermicularis.*	*Morchella esculenta.*
" *inæqualis.*	" *deliciosa.*
" *pistillaris.*	

Canned Tomatoes.—To a pint of tomatoes add butter twice the size of an egg, some pepper, very little salt, and a tablespoonful of sugar. Boil about five minutes. Put some bread crumbs or toast in a dish, and pour tomatoes over them. Butter can be omitted. Some do not like sugar in tomatoes.

Canned Corn.—Same as tomatoes; but omit sugar and bread. Add a cup of milk, if you have it.

Miscellaneous Vegetables.—Since campers very seldom have any other fresh vegetables than potatoes and onions, I will not take up space with special recipes for others. The following time-table may some time be useful:

Boiling of Vegetables.

Asparagus	20 to 25 minutes	
Cabbage	20 " 25 "	
Carrots	30 " 40 "	
Cauliflower	20 " 25 "	
Corn (green)	15 " 20 "	
Beans (string)	25 " 30 "	
Beans (Lima)	30 " 35 "	
Beans (navy, dried)	2½ " 4 hours	
Beets	30 to 40 minutes	
Onions	30 " 40 "	
Parsnips	30 " 35 "	
Peas (green)	20 "	
Potatoes (new)	20 "	
Potatoes (old)	30 " 40 "	
Spinach	20 " 25 "	
Turnips	30 " 35 "	

SOUPS.

When Napoleon said that "soup makes the soldier," he meant thick, substantial soup—soup that sticks to the ribs—not mere broths or meat extracts, which are fit only for invalids or to coax an indifferent stomach. "Soup," says Nessmuk, "requires time, and a solid basis of the right material. Venison is the basis, and the best material is the bloody part of the deer, where the bullet went through. We used to throw this away;

we have learned better. Cut about four pounds of the bloody meat into convenient pieces, and wipe them as clean as possible with leaves or a damp cloth, but don't wash them. Put the meat into a five-quart kettle nearly filled with water, and raise it to a lively boiling pitch."

Here I must interfere. It is far better to bring the water gradually to a boil and then at once hang the kettle high over the fire where it will only keep up a moderate bubbling. There let it simmer at least two hours—better half a day. It is impossible to hasten the process. Furious boiling would ruin both the soup and the meat.

Nessmuk continues: "Have ready a three-tined fork made from a branch of birch or beech, and with this test the meat from time to time; when it parts readily from the bones, slice in a large onion. Pare six large, smooth potatoes, cut five of them into quarters, and drop them into the kettle; scrape the sixth one into the soup for thickening. Season with salt and white pepper to taste. When, by skirmishing with the wooden fork, you can fish up bones with no meat on them, the soup is cooked, and the kettle may be set aside to cool."

Any kind of game may be used in a similar way, provided that none but lean meat be used. Soup is improved by first soaking the chopped-up meat in cold water, and using this water to boil in thereafter. Soup should be skimmed for some time after it has started simmering, to remove grease and scum.

To any one who knows *petite marmite* or *poule-au-pot*, these simple directions will seem barbarous —and so they are; but barbarism has its compensations. A really first-class soup cannot be made without a full day's previous preparation and the resources of a city grocery. Mulligatawny, for example, requires thirty-two varieties of spices and other condiments. No start can be made with any standard soup until one has a supply of "stock" made of veal or beef, mutton or poultry, by long simmering and skimming and straining.

In camp, stock can be made expeditiously by cutting one or two pounds of venison into thin slices, then into dice, cover with cold water, boil gently twenty minutes, take from the fire, skim, and strain. A tolerable substitute is Liebig's beef extract dissolved in water.

Onion, cloves, mace, celery seed, salt, and red or white pepper, are used for seasoning. Sassafras leaves, dried before the fire and powdered, make the gumbo *filé* of the creoles. Recipes for, a few simple, nourishing soups, are given below:

Squirrel Soup.—Put the squirrels (not less than three) in a gallon of cold water, with a scant tablespoonful of salt. Cover the pot closely, bring to the bubbling point, and then simmer gently until the meat begins to be tender. Then add whatever vegetables you have. When the meat has boiled to a rag, remove the bones. Thicken the soup with a piece of butter rubbed to a smooth paste in flour. Season to taste.

Croutons for Soup.—Slice some stale bread half an inch thick, remove crust, and cut bread into half-inch dice. Fry these, a few at a time, in deep fat of the "blue smoke" temperature, until they are golden brown. Drain free from grease, and add to each plate of soup when serving. (See also page 114.)

Tomato Soup.—Take a quart can of tomatoes

and a sliced onion. Stew twenty minutes. Meantime boil a quart of milk. Rub to a paste two tablespoonfuls each of flour and butter, and add to the boiling milk, stirring until it thickens. Now season the tomatoes with a teaspoonful of sugar, a little salt, and pepper. Then stir into the tomatoes one-half teaspoonful baking soda (to keep milk from curdling), add the boiling milk, stir quickly, and serve.

Bean Soup.—Boil with pork, as previously directed, until the beans are tender enough to crack open; then take out the pork and mash the beans into a paste. Return pork to kettle, add a cup of flour mixed thin with cold water, stirring it in slowly as the kettle simmers. Boil slowly an hour longer, stirring frequently so that it may not scorch. Season with little salt but plenty of pepper.

Pea Soup.—Wash well one pint of split peas, cover with cold water, and let them soak over night. In the morning put them in a kettle with close-fitting cover. Pour over them three quarts cold water, adding one-half pound lean bacon or ham cut into dice, one teaspoonful salt, and some pepper. When the soup begins to boil, skim the froth from the surface. Cook slowly three to four hours, stirring occasionally till the peas are all dissolved, and adding a little more boiling water to keep up the quantity as it boils away. Let it get quite thick. Just before serving, drop in small squares of toasted bread or biscuits, adding quickly while the bread is hot. Vegetables may be added one-half hour before the soup is done.

Condensed Soups.—Follow directions on wrapper.

Skilligalee.—The best thing in a fixed camp is

the stock-pot. A large covered pot or enameled pail is reserved for this and nothing else. Into it go all the clean fag-ends of game—heads, tails, wings, feet, giblets, large bones—also the left-overs of fish, flesh, and fowl, of any and all sorts of vegetables, rice, or other cereals, macaroni, stale bread, everything edible except fat and grease. This pot is always kept hot. Its flavors are for-ever changing, but ever welcome. It is always ready, day or night, for the hungry varlet who missed connections or who wants a bite between meals. No cook who values his peace of mind will fail to have skilly simmering at all hours.

CHAPTER XI.

BEVERAGES AND DESSERTS.

COFFEE.—To have coffee in perfection the berry must be freshly roasted and freshly ground. This can be done with frying-pan and pistol-butt; yet few but old-timers take the trouble.

There are two ways of making good coffee in an ordinary pot. (1) Put coffee in pot with cold water (one heaped tablespoonful freshly ground to one pint, or more, if canned ground) and hang over fire. Watch it, and when water first begins to bubble, remove pot from fire and let it stand five minutes. Settle grounds with a tablespoonful of cold water poured down spout. Do not let the coffee boil. Boiling extracts the tannin, and drives off the volatile aroma which is the most precious gift of superior berries. (2) Bring water to hard boil, remove from fire, and quickly put coffee in. Cover tightly and let steep ten minutes. A better way, when you have a seamless vessel that will stand dry heat, is to put coffee in, place over gentle fire to roast until aroma begins to rise, pour boiling water over the coffee, cover tightly, and set aside.

Tea.—Pour boiling water over tea (one heaped teaspoonful tea to the pint), cover tightly, and steep *away* from fire *four minutes by the watch.* Then, if you have no percolator, strain into sep-

135

arate vessel. If tea is left steeping more than five or six minutes the result is a liquor that will tan skin into leather.

To boil tea is—well, it is like watering a rare vintage. You know what the old Colonel said: "My friend, if you put water in that wine, God'll never forgive you!"

Chocolate.—For each quart of boiling water scrape up four tablespoonfuls of chocolate. Boil until dissolved. Then add half a pint milk. Stir with a peeled stick until milk has boiled up once. Let each man sweeten his own cup.

DESSERTS.

Dried Fruit.—Evaporated or dried apples, apricots, peaches, prunes, etc., are misprized, underrated, by most people from not knowing how to prepare them. The common way is to put the fruit on to stew without previous soaking, and then boil from one-half hour to two hours until it is more or less pulpy. It is then flat and insipid, besides unattractive to the eye.

There is a much better way. Soak the fruit at least over night, in clear cold water—just enough to cover. If time permits, soak it from twenty-four to thirty-six hours. This restores the fruit to its original size and flavor. It is good to eat, then, without cooking. To stew, merely simmer gently a few minutes in the water in which the fruit was soaked. This water carries much of the fruit's flavor, and is invaluable for sauce.

California prunes prepared in this way need no sugar. Dried apples and peaches have none of the rank taste by which they are unfavorably known, but resemble the canned fruit. Apricots properly soaked are especially good.

Jelly from Dried Fruit.—I was present when a Southern mountain woman did some "experiencin'," with nothing to guide her but her own wits. The result was a discovery of prime value to us campers. Here are the details—any one can follow them:

Wash one pound of evaporated apples (or common sun-dried apples of the country) in two waters. Cover with boiling water, and put them on to stew. Add boiling water as required to keep them covered. Cook until fruit is soft (about half an hour). Strain off all the juice (cheesecloth is convenient), and measure it. There will be, probably, a quart. Put this juice on the fire and add half its own measure of granulated sugar (say a scant pound—but measure it, to make sure of the proportion).

Now boil this briskly in a broad, uncovered vessel, without stirring or skimming, until the juice gets syrupy. The time varies according to quality of fruit—generally about twenty minutes after coming to a full boil. When the thickened juice begins to "flop," test it by letting a few drops drip from a spoon. When the drops thicken and adhere to the spoon, the syrup is done. There will be a little more than a pint. Pour it out. As soon as it cools it will be jelly, as good as if made from fresh fruit and much better than what is commonly sold in the stores.

The apples remaining can be spiced and used as sauce, or made into pies or turnovers, or into apple butter by beating smooth, adding a teacupful of sugar, spicing, and cooking again for fifteen or twenty minutes.

If preferred, a second run of jelly can be made from the same apples. Cover again with boil-

ing water, stew about fifteen minutes, add sugar
by measure, as before. This will take less boiling
than the first juice (about seven minutes).
Enough jelly will result to make nearly or quite
a quart, all told, from one pound of dried apples
and about one and one-half pounds of sugar.

Apricots or any other tart dried fruit can be
used instead of apples. Sweet fruit will not do,
unless lemon juice or real apple vinegar is added.

Wild Fruits.—American wild fruits ripen as
follows:

May—June.

Chickasaw Plum (to July).
Wild Strawberries.

June—July.

Woolly-leaved Buckthorn.
Dewberry.
Service-berry (June-berry).
Shad-bush.

July.

May Apple.

July—August.

Blackberries (some in Sep.).
Bilberries.
Blueberries.
Huckleberries.
Buffalo-berry.
Choke Cherry.
Wild Black Currant.
Wild Gooseberries.
Riverside Grape (to Oct.).
Wild Raspberries (to Sep.).
Salmon-berry.
Silver-berry.

August.

Sand Cherry.
Western Wild Cherry.
Wild Red Cherry.
Elderberry.
Sand Grape.
Canada Plum.
Porter's Plum.

August—September.

Barberry.
Cranberries.

Wild Black Cherry.
Fox Grape.
Wild Red Plum (to Oct.).
Snowberry.

September.

Carolina Buckthorn.

September—October.

Wild Crab-apples.
Summer Grape.
Haws.
Beach Plum.
Wild Goose Plum.
Large-fruited Thorn.
Scarlet Thorn.

October.

Missouri Grape.
Black Thorn.

October—November.

Frost Grape.

Edible After Frost.

Pawpaw.
Persimmon.

Pie.—It is not to be presumed that a mere male camper can make a good pie-crust in the regular way; but it is easy to make a wholesome and very fair pie-crust in an irregular way, which is as follows: Make a glorified biscuit dough by mixing thoroughly 1 pint flour, 1 teaspoonful baking powder, ½ teaspoonful salt, rubbing in 4 heaped tablespoonfuls of lard (better still, half-and-half of butter and lard), and making into a soft dough with cold water. In doing this, observe the rules given under *Biscuit.* The above quantity is enough for a pie filling an 8x12 reflector pan. Roll the dough into a thin sheet, as thin as you can handle, and do the rolling as gently as you can.

From this sheet cut a piece large enough for bottom crust and lay it in the greased pan. The sheet should be big enough to lap over edge of pan. Into this put your fruit (dried fruit is

previously stewed and mashed), and add sugar
and spice to taste. Then, with great circumspec-
tion and becoming reverence, lay on top of all this
your upper crust. Now, with your thumb, press
the edges of upper and lower crust together all
around, your thumb-prints leaving scallops around
the edge. Trim off by running a knife around
edge of pan. Then prick a number of small slits
in the top crust, here and there, to give a vent
to the stem when the fruit boils. Bake as you
would biscuits.

Note that this dough contains baking powder,
and that it will swell. Don't give the thing a
name until it is baked; then, if you have made the
crust too thick for a pie, call it a cobbler, or a
shortcake, and the boys, instead of laughing at
you, will ask for more.

Doughnuts.—Mix 1 quart of flour with 1 teaspoonful of salt, 1 tablespoonful of baking powder, and 1 pint of granulated sugar, and ½ nutmeg grated. Make a batter of this with 4 beaten
eggs and enough milk to make smooth. Beat thoroughly and add enough flour to make a soft
dough. Roll out into a sheet ½ inch thick and
cut into rings or strips, which may be twisted into
shape. Fry in very hot fat; turn when necessary. Drain and serve hot.

Snits und Knepp.—This is a Pennsylvania-
Dutch dish, and a good one for campers. Take
some dried apples and soak them over night. Boil
until tender. Prepare knepp as directed for pot-
pie dough, only make a thick batter of it instead
of a dough. It is best to add an egg and use
no shortening. Drop the batter into the pan of
stewing apples, a large spoonful at a time, not
fast enough to check the boiling. Boil about ½

hour. Season with butter, sugar, and cinnamon.

Fruit Cobbler.—Make up your dough as directed under *Pie,* excepting omit baking powder, and use ½ pound of mixed butter and lard to 2 pints flour. Mix with coldest spring water, and have your hands cold. After putting under crust in greased pan, pour in scant 3 pints of fruit, which may be either fresh, canned, or evaporated (soaked as explained under *Dried Fruits*), leaving out the free juice. Cover with upper crust, bake brown, and serve with milk or pudding sauce.

Puddings are either baked in an oven or reflector, or boiled in a cloth bag. Baked puddings are quickest and easiest to manage. A few examples of simple puddings are given below. They may be varied indefinitely, according to materials available. Deep tin pudding pans are convenient to bake in. Snow may be substituted for eggs (see page 111).

Rice Pudding.—Mix 1 pint cold boiled rice with 1 quart milk and sugar to taste. Put in a well-greased pan, dust nutmeg or cinnamon over the top, and bake slowly one hour. Seeded raisins are an agreeable addition, and a couple of eggs make the pudding richer. Mix them in before baking. To stone them, keep them in lukewarm water during the process.

Fruit Pudding.—Line a deep dish or pan, well greased, with slices of buttered bread. Then put in a layer of fruit, dusting it with sugar and dotting with small lumps of butter. Repeat these alternate layers until the dish is full, the last layer being bread. Bake ½ to ¾ hour, with moderate heat. Eat hot, with the sweet sauce given below.

Cottage Pudding.—
    1 pint flour,
    ½ pint sugar,
    ½ pint milk,
    2 heaped tablespoonfuls butter,
    1 egg,
    2 teaspoonfuls baking powder,
    Grated rind of a lemon.

Mix thoroughly the flour and baking powder. Rub the butter and sugar to ·a cream, add the milk and egg beaten together; then the lemon rind. Add this to the flour and mix well. Butter a pan well to prevent scorching and dredge it with flour or powdered bread-crumbs. Pour in the batter, and bake about half an hour in hot oven.

A richer pudding is made by using one-half pound butter and two eggs.

A cupful of stoned raisins, minced figs, or dates, added to the batter, converts this into a good fruit pudding. Nutmeg, cinnamon, or other flavoring may be substituted for lemon.

Batter Pudding.—
    ½ pint flour,
    1 pint milk,
    1 heaped tablespoonful butter,
    6 eggs.

Beat flour and milk into a smooth batter. Then add the eggs, beaten light. Stir all well together, adding the butter in tiny lumps. Dip a clean cloth bag into hot water, dredge it with flour, pour the batter into this, tie up firmly, and put into plenty of boiling water. Keep this boiling steadily for an hour. Then dip the bag quickly in cold water and remove cloth with care not to break the pudding. Serve very hot, with a sauce.

Plain Plum Duff.—
    1 quart flour,
    1 heaped teaspoonful baking powder,
    2 tablespoonfuls sugar,
    1 ℔. seeded raisins.
    ¾ ℔. suet (or see below).

Venison suet chopped fine, or the fat of salt pork minced up, will serve. Marrow is better than either. Mix the dry ingredients intimately. Then make up with half a pint of water. Put this into a cloth bag prepared as in the preceding recipe. Since suet puddings swell considerably, the bag must be large enough to allow for this. Place in enough boiling water to cover, and do not let it check boiling until done (about two hours). Add boiling water as required to keep the bag covered. Turn the bag upside down when pudding begins to set, or the fruit will all go to the bottom; turn it around now and then to prevent scorching against sides of pot. When done, manipulate it like cottage pudding. Serve with sweet sauce.

A richer duff can be made by spicing and adding molasses, or the rind and juice of a lemon.

Sweet Sauce for Puddings.—Melt a little butter, sweeten it to taste, and flavor with grated lemon rind, nutmeg, or cinnamon.

Brandy Sauce.—Butter twice the size of an egg is to be beaten to a cream with a pint of sugar and a tablespoonful of flour. Add a gill of brandy. Set the cup in a dish of boiling water and beat until the sauce froths.

Fruit Sauce.—Boil almost any fresh fruit until it is quite soft. Squeeze it through cheesecloth, sweeten to taste, heat it, and pour the sauce over your pudding. Spices may be added during the final heating.

APPENDIX.

COOK'S MEASURES.

45 drops water=1 teaspoonful=1 fluidram.
2 teaspoonfuls=1 dessertspoonful.
4 teaspoonfuls=1 tablespoonful.
2 tablespoonfuls=1 fluidounce.
4 tablespoonfuls=1 wineglassful.
8 tablespoonfuls=1 gill.
2 gills=1 cup.
4 gills=1 pint (1 ℔. water).
2 pints=1 quart (1 ℔. flour).
4 quarts=1 gallon.
2 gallons (dry)=1 peck.
4 pecks (dry)=1 bushel.

OUTFITTER'S DATA.

Baking powder...................1 ℔.=1¼ pints.
Beans, dried..................... 1 qt.=1¾ ℔s.
Coffee, roasted whole............1 qt.=10 oz.
Corn meal.......................1 qt.=1¼ ℔s.
Flour........................... 1 qt.=1 ℔.
Macaroni........................1 ℔.=8⅞x2⅜x2⅜ in.
Oatmeal.........................1 qt.=⅝ ℔.
Peas, split..................... 1 qt.=1¾ ℔s.
Rice............................ 1 qt.=2 ℔s.
Salt, dry.......................1 qt.=1⅞ ℔s.

Soda crackers are about 3 times as bulky as bread, weight for weight.

144

Sugar, granulated....... 1 qt.=1¾ ℔s.
Tea..................... 1 qt.=½ ℔.
Bacon, breakfast........ 1 flitch=5-8 ℔s., average.
Salt pork............... 1 side=30-40 ℔s., average.
Salt pork............... 1 belly=20 ℔s., average.
Butter, closely packed.. 1 ℔.=1 pint.
Butter, creamery........ 1 ℔.=4⅝x2½x2½ in.
Eggs, desiccated......... 1 ℔.=6x3x3 in.=4 doz. fresh.
Eggs, fresh............. 10 medium or 8 large=1 ℔.
Lard.................... 3 ℔. pail=5x5 in.
Lard.................... 5 ℔. pail=6x6 in.
Milk, evaporated........ 7 oz. can=2½x2½ in.
Milk, evaporated........ 12 oz. can=3⅜x3 in.
Milk, evaporated........ 1 ℔. can=4⅜x3 in.
Apples, evaporated...... 1 ℔. (14 oz.)=7⅛x4½x2 in.
Apples, evaporated...... 1 peck=6 ℔s.
Corn, canned............ 1 can=2¼ ℔s.=4⅝x3⅜ in.
Fruit, canned, small can, same as corn.
Fruit, canned, large can, same as tomatoes.
Tomatoes, canned........ 1 can=2½ ℔s.=4⅞x4⅛ in.
Lemons.................. 1 doz.=2 ℔s.=2 qts.
Raisins, stemmed........ 1 ℔.=1⅓ pints.
Carrots................. 1 qt.=1¼ ℔.
Onions.................. 1 qt.=1 ℔.
Potatoes................ 1 peck=15 ℔s.
Sweet Potatoes.......... 1 peck=14 ℔s.

THE END.

INDEX.

147

Made in the USA
Lexington, KY
14 July 2013